CROCHET
A FLOWER BOUQUET

35 crochet patterns for handmade flowers and foliage

Li Li

DAVID & CHARLES
—PUBLISHING—

www.davidandcharles.com

CONTENTS

Introduction 4
Tools & Materials 6

Focal Flowers 8
Classic Rose 10
Thai Rose 13
Hyacinth 16
Peony 18
Sunflower 22
Lily 24
Common Rose 26
Epiphyllum 29

Secondary Flowers 32
Tulip 34
Freesia 36
Chinese Lantern Lily 39
Daisy 42
Carnation 44
Lily of the Valley 46
Cosmos 48
Plum Blossom 50
Moth Orchid 53
Zephyr Lily 56

Filler Flowers 58
Winter Berry 60
Spray Rose 62
Baby's Breath 64
Sweet Pea 66
Morning Glory 69
Bell Flower 72
Calla Lily 74

Foliage 76
Fern Leaf 78
Ginkgo Leaf 81
Common Leaf 84
Orchid Leaf 86
Northern Sea Oats 88
Mint Leaf 90
Cordyline Fruticosa 92
Long Eucalyptus 94
Broad Eucalyptus 96
Maple Leaf 98

Bouquet Ideas 100
Wedding Bouquet 102
Classic Roses Bouquet 106
Congratulations Bouquet 110
Happy Home Display 114
Cascade Bouquet 118

Stitches & Techniques 122
About the Author, Thanks & Suppliers 126
Index 127

INTRODUCTION

There's something magical about turning a simple strand of yarn into a vibrant, lifelike flower. The delicate curves of a rose petal, the soft sweep of a lily's stamen, the intricate folds of a peony blossom — all recreated with nothing more than a crochet hook and a bit of patience. We're drawn to the beauty of real flowers, but the impermanence of their blooms can feel bittersweet. So here we set out on a journey to create something that will last, something that will keep its beauty for years, not just days.

In this book, I invite you to explore an enchanting world where crochet meets floristry. This isn't just a book about making flowers; it's about capturing the essence of nature's most beautiful blooms and arranging them into bouquets that tell a story, express an emotion or brighten someone's day. I believe that every bouquet should have its own personality and its own life, even when the flowers are made of yarn.

This book is for those who love beautiful things. Here, you'll learn how to crochet 35 different flowers — from the bold, attention-grabbing focal blooms to the delicate filler flowers and lush greenery that bring everything together. I'll also guide you through the process of creating five themed bouquets, perfect for those special moments: Valentine's Day, Mother's Day, graduations, weddings, and more.

So, grab your hook, choose your yarn, and let's get started. Together, we'll create bouquets that never fade, that bring joy and beauty into any space, and that are a true testament to the art of crochet.

Li Li

TOOLS & MATERIALS

I always keep the following tools and supplies within easy reach in my studio. These are the essentials you will need to complete the projects in this book.

YARN

Milk cotton yarn:

4-ply cotton yarn, 60% cotton, 40% acrylic, about 2mm, suitable for 1.5mm (US 8/7/2) to 2mm (US 4) hooks.

5-ply, 60% cotton, 40% acrylic, thicker than 4-ply, about 3mm, suitable for 2mm (US 4) to 3.5mm (US E-4) hook. With same size hook, crochet flowers made with 5-ply yarn will be bigger than those made with 4-ply.

Each project includes the quantity of yarn you will need – the minimum is 2g (⅛oz) and the maximum is 35g (1¼oz). The 'ounce' conversions are too small to be exact but we have rounded each one up to the nearest ¼oz so you will always have more than you need if you decide to work in ounces.

HOOKS

Size 1.5mm (US 8/7/2) and 2mm (US 4). The finer the hook, the more delicate the crocheted flower. In the US, you will find standard crochet hooks sizes and steel crochet hook sizes, with the steel sizes applying to small and very small hooks. I have used steel sizes here.

FLORAL STEM

This is a type of coated iron wire frequently used in floral design. It comes in various thicknesses and lengths. As it offers good flexibility, it can be bent freely. I commonly use:

2mm diameter, 40cm (16in) length. This makes a stem suitable for small and medium-size flowers, such as tulips, bell flowers, and foliage.

3mm diameter, 40cm (16in) length. This makes a stem suitable for heavy flowers, such as Thai roses, lilies, and hyacinths.

FLORAL WIRE

This thin iron wire is usually sold in rolls. You can cut it to any length with scissors and use it to shape flowers and leaves. It's commonly used in thicknesses ranging from 0.3mm to 0.8mm, with different sizes used for the following purposes:

0.3mm to 0.4mm: Used to fix flower centers, such lily stamens, and for shaping small leaves.

0.5mm: The most commonly used size, suitable for shaping petals and leaves of medium flowers, such as tulips and plum blossoms.

0.6mm to 0.8mm: Suitable for shaping large petals and leaves, such as those of a sunflower.

To crochet over floral wire, cut a piece of wire that is about twice the length of the finished petal or leaf. This way, you will have extra wire left over to secure your stitches. Crochet the foundation chain as per the pattern, then insert the wire into the last stitch of the foundation chain. Use your hand to hold the wire down, making sure it rests on top of the stitch and is parallel to it. Continue crocheting, wrapping the wire in with the stitches. When you've finished crocheting, bend and adjust any excess wire as needed or wrap it around the stem. You can adjust the wire to shape the leaves or petals for a more natural look.

HOT GLUE

Hot glue and a hot glue gun are used for assembling petals and securing wire ends. Insert the hot glue sticks into the glue gun, plug it in, and heat it before use. Handle with care to avoid burns.

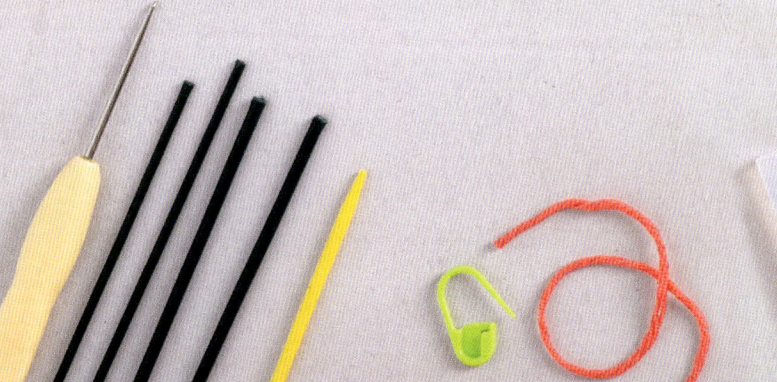

OTHER ACCESSORIES

Small, sharp scissors: Ideal for cutting yarn with precision.
Tapestry needles: Best for sewing seams due to their blunt tips and large eyes.
Stitch markers: Slipped onto a specific stitch or row, as an aid to counting.
Needle-nose pliers: for bending thicker wire.
Perforated pearls and faux flower stamens: Used as the centers of small flowers such as baby's breath and plum blossoms.
Fiberfill stuffing: to add dimension to elements such as buds and flower centers.
Artificial stamens: for completing flowers such as lilies.

FLOWER TERMINOLOGY

Some patterns ask you to make a calyx (for example, Common Rose) or pistils (Lily). A calyx is the outer whorl of leaves found below a flower's petals. Pistils are the central reproductive parts of flowers where seeds and pollen are produced.

TERMINOLOGY

This book is written using US crochet terms. Please refer to the table below for UK equivalents.

US TERM	UK TERM
Single crochet	Double crochet
Half double crochet	Half treble crochet
Double crochet	Treble crochet
Treble crochet	Double treble crochet
Double treble crochet	Triple treble crochet

ABBREVIATIONS

*	repeat the instructions following the single asterisk as directed
[ ]	work instructions within the brackets as many times as directed
BLO	back loop only
ch	chain
ch-sp	chain space
dc	double crochet
dc2tog	double crochet two stitches together
dtr	double treble
FLO	front loop only
FPsc	front post single crochet
hdc	half double crochet
Rnd(s)	Round(s)
RS	right side
sc	single crochet
sc2tog	single crochet two stitches together
slst	slip stitch
st(s)	stitch(es)
tr	treble crochet
tr2tog	treble crochet two stitches together
WS	wrong side
yo	yarn over
1ch-picot	1-chain picot stitch
2ch-picot	2-chain picot stitch
3ch-picot	3-chain picot stitch
BPsc	back post single crochet

FOCAL FLOWERS

The attention-grabbing stars of the arrangement are usually the most prominent and eye-catching flowers. Thanks to bold colors, delicate details, or architectural shapes, they draw the most attention. As perennial favourites, these are often the reason for choosing a particular bouquet.

Classic Rose

YARN

Cotton or cotton blend, 4-ply in maroon (30g / 1oz) and green (10g / ½oz)

HOOK

2mm (US 4)

MATERIALS

0.5mm floral wire for leaves: 3 x 20cm (8in) lengths

2mm floral stem: 1 x 40cm (16in) length

Hot glue gun

PATTERN NOTE:

This pattern uses the amigurumi method of working in a spiral. Join each round with a slst into the top of the first sc. It will help to use a stitch marker in the first stitch of the round, so that you know when you have completed the round. Move the marker up as you work.

SMALL PETAL #1
(MAKE 1)

Using maroon, make a magic ring.

Rnd 1 (RS): 1 ch (does not count as a st throughout), 6 sc into ring, join. (6 sts)

Rnd 2: 1 ch, [2 sc in the next st] 6 times, join. (12 sts)

Rnd 3: 1 ch, [1 sc, 2 sc in the next st] 6 times, join. (18 sts)

Rnd 4: 1 ch, [2 sc, 2 sc in the next st] 6 times, join. (24 sts)

Rnd 5: 1 ch, [3 sc, 2 sc in the next st] 6 times, join. (30 sts)

Rnd 6: 1 ch, [4 sc, 2 sc in the next st] 6 times, join. (36 sts)

Rnd 7: 1 ch, 10 sc, [4 sc, 2 sc in the next st] 3 times, 2 sc in the next st, 10 sc, join. (40 sts)

Fasten off and weave in the end.

SMALL PETAL #2
(MAKE 1)

Rnds 1–7: Using maroon, work as for small petal #1.

Rnd 8: 1 ch, 10 sc, [5 sc, 2 sc in the next st] 3 times, 2 sc in the next st, 11 sc, join. (44 sts)

Fasten off and weave in the end.

SMALL PETAL #3
(MAKE 1)

Rnds 1–8: Using maroon, work as for small petal #2.

Rnd 9: 1 ch, 11 sc, [6 sc, 2 sc in the next st] 3 times, 2 sc in the next st, 11 sc, join. (48 sts)

Fasten off and weave in the end.

MEDIUM PETAL
(MAKE 3)

Rnds 1–9: Using maroon, work as for small petal #3.

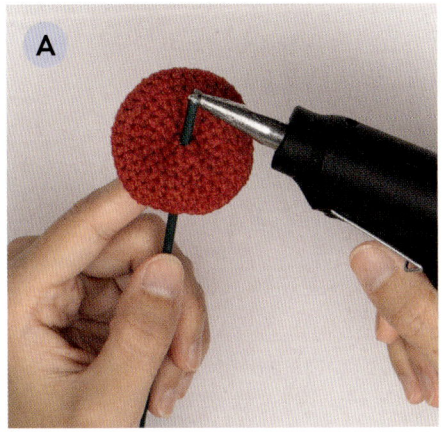
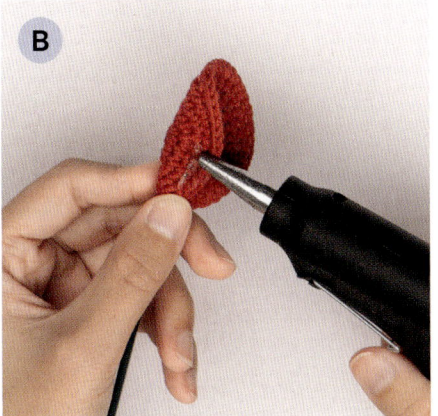
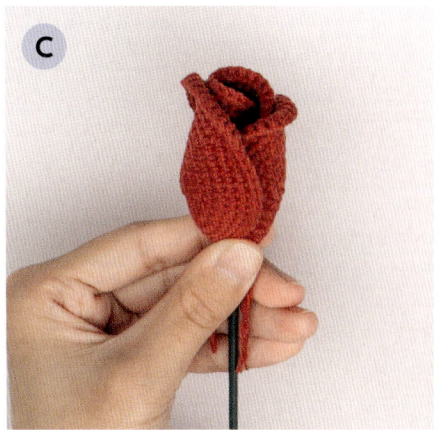

Rnd 10: 1 ch, 11 sc, 2 sc in the next st, 3 sc, [1 sc, 1 ch, 1 sc] all into the next st, 3 sc, 2 sc in the next st, 3 sc, [1 sc, 2 ch, 1 sc] all into the next st, 3 sc, 2 sc in the next st, 3 sc, [1 sc, 1 ch, 1 sc] all into the next st, 3 sc, 2 sc in the next st, 12 sc, join. (55 sts)

Fasten off and weave in the end.

LARGE PETAL
(MAKE 3)

Rnds 1–10: Using maroon, work as for medium petal.

Rnd 11: 1 ch, 12 sc, 2 sc in the next st, 4 sc, [1 sc, 1 ch, 1 sc] all into the next st, 4 sc, 2 sc in the next st, 4 sc, [1 sc, 2 ch, 1 sc] all into the next st, 4 sc, 2 sc in the next st, 4 sc, [1 sc, 1 ch, 1 sc] all into the next st, 4 sc, 2 sc in the next st, 12 sc, join. (62 sts)

Fasten off and weave in the end.

BIG LEAF
(MAKE 1)

Using green, ch 13.

Rnd 1: Starting in the 2nd ch from hook, 11 sc, 3 sc in the next st, rotate to work into opposite side of ch, 10 sc, 2 sc in the next st, join. (26 sts)

Rnd 2: 1 ch, 1 sc, 1 hdc, 1 dc, 6 tr, 1 dc, 1 hdc, 1 sc, 3 sc in the next st, 1 sc, 1 hdc, 1 dc, 6 tr, 1 dc, 1 hdc, 2 sc, join. (28 sts)

Rnd 3: Working over floral wire, 1 ch, [1 sc, 2 ch] 13 times, [1 sc, 3 ch, 1 sc] all into the next st, [2 ch, 1 sc] 14 times, join. (29 sts)

Fasten off and weave in the end.

SMALL LEAF
(MAKE 2)

Using green, ch 11.

Rnd 1: Starting in the 2nd ch from hook, 9 sc, 3 sc in the next st, rotate to work in opposite side of ch, 8 sc, 2 sc in the next st, join. (22 sts)

Rnd 2: 1 ch, 1 sc, 1 hdc, 1 dc, 4 tr, 1 dc, 1 hdc, 1 sc, 3 sc in next st, 1 sc, 1 hdc, 1 dc, 4 tr, 1 dc, 1 hdc, 2 sc, join. (24 sts)

Rnd 3: Working over floral wire, 1 ch, [1 sc, 2 ch] 11 times, [1 sc, 2 ch, 1 sc] all into the next st, [2 ch, 1 sc] 12 times, join. (25 sts)

Fasten off and weave in the end.

CALYX
(MAKE 1)

Using green, make a magic ring.

Rnd 1: 1 ch, 6 sc into ring, join. (6 sts)

Rnd 2: 1 ch, [2 sc in the next st] 6 times, join. (12 sts)

Rnd 3: 1 ch, [1 sc, 2 sc in the next st] 6 times, join. (18 sts)

Rnd 4: 1 ch, 18 sc, join. (18 sts)

Rnd 5: * 13 ch, starting in the 2nd ch from hook, 1 slst, 2 sc, 2 hdc, 3 dc, 4 tr, skip st at bottom of ch and next st, 1 slst. Repeat from * 5 more times.

Fasten off and weave in the end.

Assembly

1. Insert the stem into the center of the smallest petal (A) and secure it with glue, ensuring the petal is wrapped around the stem.

2. Layer on the #2 and #3 small petals one by one, using glue to fix them around the previous petals (B, C).

3. Repeat the above steps, gradually wrapping the three medium petals and three large petals until the flower takes shape (D, E).

4. Insert the stem through the center of the calyx and use glue to secure each section of the calyx onto the petals (F).

5. Starting from the base of the calyx, begin wrapping the stem with green thread, ensuring the wire is fully covered.

6. Wrap two small leaves around each side of the large leaf (G) and secure them to the stem about a quarter of the way down (H).

7. Continue wrapping the stem with thread to the bottom, secure with glue, and cut the yarn (I).

Thai Rose

YARN
Cotton or cotton blend, 4-ply in dark pink (35g / 1¼oz) and green (10g / ½oz)

HOOK
2mm (US 4)

MATERIALS
0.5mm floral wire for leaves: 2 x 20cm (8in) lengths

3mm floral stem: 1 x 40cm (16in) length

Hot glue gun

PATTERN NOTE:
This pattern uses the amigurumi method of working in a spiral. Join each round with a slst into the top of the first sc. It will help to use a stitch marker in the first stitch of the round, so that you know when you have completed the round. Move the marker up as you work.

SMALL PETAL
(MAKE 4)

Using dark pink, make a magic ring.

Rnd 1 (RS): 1 ch (does not count as a st throughout), 5 sc into ring, join. (5 sts)

Rnd 2: 1 ch, [2 sc in the next st] 5 times, join. (10 sts)

Rnd 3: 1 ch, [1 sc, 2 sc in the next st] 5 times, join. (15 sts)

Rnd 4: 1 ch, [1 sc, 2 sc in the next st, 1 sc] 5 times, join. (20 sts)

Rnd 5: 1 ch, [3 sc, 2 sc in the next st] 5 times, join. (25 sts)

Rnd 6: 1 ch, [2 sc, 2 sc in the next st, 2 sc] 5 times, join. (30 sts)

Rnd 7: 1 ch, 11 sc, 2 hdc in the next st, 2 hdc, 2 hdc in the next st, 2 hdc, 2 hdc in the next st, 12 sc, join. (33 sts)

Rnd 8: 1 ch, 11 sc, [2 dc in 1 st] 10 times, 12 sc, join. (43 sts)

Rnd 9: 3 ch (counts as 1 dc), turn, 2 dc in the next st, 1 dc, leave remaining sts unworked. (4 sts)

Fasten off and weave in the end.

MEDIUM PETAL
(MAKE 4)

Using dark pink, make a magic ring.

Rnd 1 (RS): 1 ch, 5 sc into ring, join. (5 sts)

Rnd 2: 1 ch, [2 sc in the next st] 5 times, join. (10 sts)

Rnd 3: 1 ch, [1 sc, 2 sc in the next st] 5 times, join. (15 sts)

Rnd 4: 1 ch, [1 sc, 2 sc in the next st, 1 sc] 5 times, join. (20 sts)

Rnd 5: 1 ch, [3 sc, 2 sc in the next st] 5 times, join. (25 sts)

Rnd 6: 1 ch, [2 sc, 2 sc in the next st, 2 sc] 5 times, join. (30 sts)

> ## Tip
>
> To stay safe when using hot glue, apply small amounts and wait for it to cool before moving on. Alternatively, stitch the flowers together for added precision.

A

Rnd 7: 1 ch, [5 sc, 2 sc in the next st] 5 times, join. (35 sts)

Rnd 8: 1 ch, 6 sc, [2 hdc in the next st, 6 hdc] 3 times, 2 hdc in the next st, 7 sc, join. (39 sts)

Rnd 9: 1 ch, 7 sc, [2 dc in the next st] 12 times, [2 dc, 2ch-picot, 2 dc] all into the next st, [2 dc in the next st] 12 times, 7 sc, join. (66 sts, 1 2ch-picot)

Rnd 10: 3 ch (counts as 1 dc), turn, 2 dc in the next st, 1 dc, leave remaining sts unworked. (4 sts)

Fasten off and weave in the end.

LARGE PETAL
(MAKE 5)

Using dark pink, make a magic ring.

Rnd 1 (RS): 1 ch, 5 sc into ring, join. (5 sts)

Rnd 2: 1 ch, [2 sc in the next st] 5 times, join. (10 sts)

Rnd 3: 1 ch, [1 sc, 2 sc in the next st] 5 times, join. (15 sts)

Rnd 4: 1 ch, [1 sc, 2 sc in the next st, 1 sc] 5 times, join. (20 sts)

Rnd 5: 1 ch, [3 sc, 2 sc in the next st] 5 times, join. (25 sts)

Rnd 6: 1 ch, [2 sc, 2 sc in the next st, 2 sc] 5 times, join. (30 sts)

Rnd 7: 1 ch, [5 sc, 2 sc in the next st] 5 times, join. (35 sts)

Rnd 8: 1 ch, [3 sc, 2 sc in the next st, 3 sc] 5 times, join. (40 sts)

Rnd 9: 7 hdc, [2 hdc in the next st, 3 hdc] 6 times, 2 hdc in 1 st, 8 hdc, join. (47 sts)

Rnd 10: 7 dc, [2 dc in the next st] 16 times, 4 dc in the next st, [2 dc in the next st] 16 times, 7 dc, join. (82 sts)

Rnd 11: 3 ch (counts as 1 dc), turn, 2 dc in the next st, 1 dc, leave remaining sts unworked. (4 sts)

Fasten off and weave in the end.

BIG LEAF

Using green, ch 15.

Rnd 1 (RS): Starting in the 2nd ch from hook, working over floral wire, 1 sc, 1 dc, 2 tr, 1 dtr, 2 dtr in the next st, 1 dtr, 2 dtr in the next st, 1 dtr, 2 tr, 1 dc, 1 hdc, 3 sc in the next st, rotate to work into opposite side of ch, 1 hdc, 1 dc, 2 tr, 1 dtr, 2 dtr in the next st, 1 dtr, 2 dtr in the next st, 1 dtr, 2 tr, 1 dc, 1 sc, join. (33 sts)

Rnd 2: [1 sc, 2 ch] 16 times, [1 sc, 3ch-picot, 1 sc] all into the next st, [1 sc, 2 ch] 16 times, join.

Fasten off and weave in the end.

SMALL LEAF
(MAKE 2)

Using green, ch 12.

Rnd 1 (RS): Starting in the 2nd ch from hook, working over floral wire, 1 sc, 1 dc, 1 tr, 2 dtr, 2 dtr in the next st, 1 dtr, 1 tr, 1 dc, 1 hdc, 3 sc in the next st, rotate to work into opposite side of ch, 1 hdc, 1 dc, 1 tr, 1 dtr, 2 dtr in the next st, 2 dtr, 1 tr, 1 dc, 1 sc, join. (25 sts)

Rnd 2: [1 sc, 2 ch] 12 times, [1 sc, 3ch-picot, 1 sc] in the next st, [1 sc, 2 ch] 12 times, join.

Fasten off and weave in the end.

CALYX
(MAKE 1)

Using green, make a magic ring.

Rnd 1 (RS): 1 ch, 5 sc into ring, join. (5 sts)

Rnd 2: 1 ch, [2 sc in the next st] 5 times, join. (10 sts)

Rnd 3: 1 ch, [1 sc, 2 sc in the next st] 5 times, join. (15 sts)

Rnd 4: 1 ch, [1 sc, 2 sc in the next st, 1 sc] 5 times, join. (20 sts)

Rnds 5–7: 1 ch, 20 sc, join.

Now work in rows.

Row 1 (RS): 1 ch, 4 sc, turn. (4 sts)

Row 2: 1 ch, 2 sc in the next st, 1 sc, 2 sc in next st, 1 sc, turn. (6 sts)

Rows 3–4: 1 ch, 6 sc, turn.

Row 5: 1 ch, 1 sc2tog, 4 sc, turn. (5 sts)

Row 6: 1 ch, 1 sc2tog, 3 sc, turn. (4 sts)

Row 7: 1 ch, 1 sc2tog, 2 sc, turn. (3 sts)

Row 8: 1 ch, 1 sc2tog, 1 sc, turn. (2 sts)

Row 9: 1 ch, 2 sc, turn.

Row 10: 1 ch, 1 sc2tog, turn. (1 st)

Row 11: 2 ch (does not count as a st), 1 hdc.

Fasten off.

* With RS facing, join yarn in next unworked st of Round 7. Repeat rows 1 to 11; repeat from * 4 more times.

Fasten off, weave in the end (A).

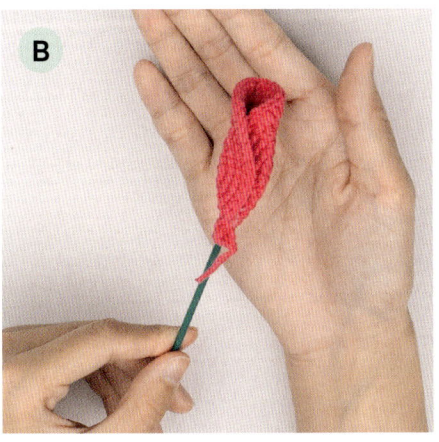
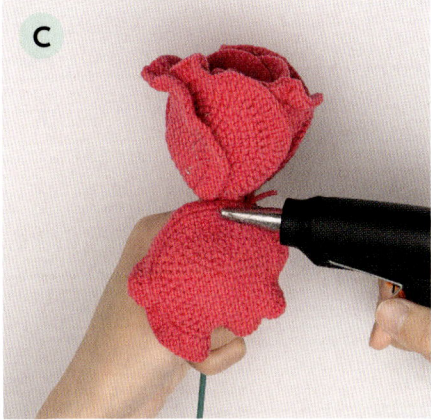
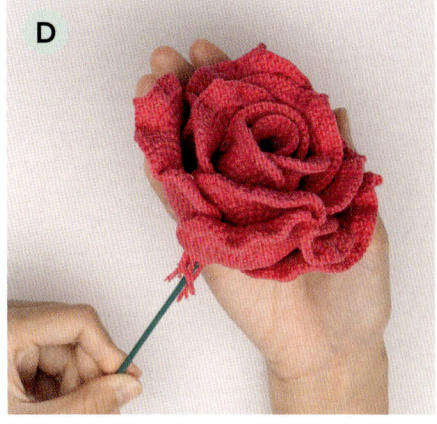

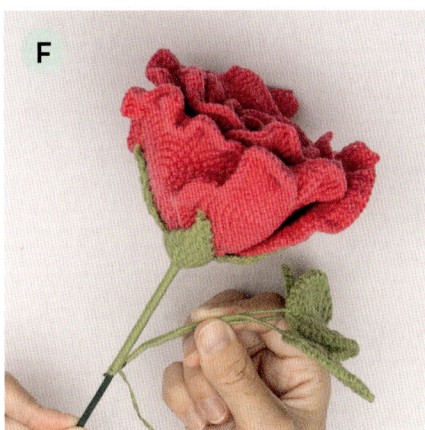

Assembly

1. Insert the floral stem into the center of the first small petal and apply a small amount of hot glue to the top of the stem. Press the petal to the stem, ensuring the hot glue firmly holds it in place (B). Wait for the glue to completely dry and cool.

2. Gradually add more petals around the first petal and the stem center, working from small to large. Each new petal should slightly overlap the edge of the previous one to create a layered effect. Apply a small amount of hot glue to the base of each new petal and press it into place (C).

3. Adjust the angle of each petal as needed to make the flower look natural and full (D).

4. Thread the calyx over the stem (E), positioning it at the base of the flower. Apply hot glue to secure it to the outer petals.

5. Begin wrapping the stem in green yarn, starting below the calyx. Place one large leaf between two small leaves, wrap with green yarn, and twist the wire to secure the leaves at the ends. Then wrap the leaves to the stem, appoximately 10cm (4in) below the petals (F).

6. Wrap the stem with green yarn from the petal base to the end (G). Apply hot glue to the end of the stem to secure the yarn, then cut the yarn.

7. Ensure all petals are securely fixed. If any petals are loose, reapply hot glue and press to secure. Make final adjustments to the overall shape of the flower, ensuring it looks natural.

Hyacinth

YARN

Cotton or cotton blend, 5-ply in white (5g / ¼oz), blue (20g / ¾oz), light blue (10g / ½oz), green (10g / ½oz)

HOOK

2mm (US 4)

MATERIALS

0.5mm floral wire for leaves: 2 x 35cm (14in) lengths

0.5mm floral wire for buds: 16 x 10cm (4in) lengths

0.5mm floral wire for flowers: 13 x 15cm (6in) lengths

3mm floral stem: 1 x 40cm (16in) length

Hot glue gun

PATTERN NOTE:

This pattern uses the amigurumi method of working in a spiral. Join each round with a slst into the top of the first sc. It will help to use a stitch marker in the first stitch of the round, so that you know when you have completed the round. Move the marker up as you work.

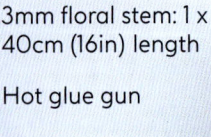

SMALL BUD

(MAKE 5)

Using white, make a magic ring.

Rnd 1: 1 ch (does not count as a st throughout), 4 sc into ring, join. (4 sts)

Rnd 2: 1 slst in every st. (4 sts)

Fasten off and weave in the end.

MEDIUM BUD

(MAKE 11)

Using light blue, make a magic ring.

Rnd 1: 1 ch (does not count as a st throughout), 6 sc into ring, join. (6 sts)

Rnd 2: 1 ch, 6 sc, join.

Rnd 3: 1 ch, [skip 1 st, 1 slst] 3 times, join. (3 sts)

Fasten off and weave in the end.

FLOWER

(MAKE 13)

Using blue, make a magic ring.

Rnd 1: 1 ch, 6 sc into ring, join. (6 sts)

Rnd 2: 1 ch, [1 sc, 2 sc in the next st] 3 times, join. (9 sts)

Rnds 3–4: 1 ch, 9 sc, join. (9 sts)

Rnd 5: 1 ch, [1 sc, 1 sc2tog] 3 times, join. (6 sts)

Rnd 6: 1 ch, * [2 dc, 1 slst] all into the next st; repeat from * 5 more times.

Fasten off and weave in the end.

LEAF

(MAKE 2)

Using green, ch 40.

Rnd 1: Starting in the 2nd ch from hook, working over floral wire, 3 sc, 3 hdc, 27 dc, 3 hdc, 2 sc, 3 sc in the next st, rotate to work into opposite side of ch, 2 sc, 3 hdc, 27 dc, 3 hdc, 3 sc, join. (79 sts)

Fasten off and weave in the end.

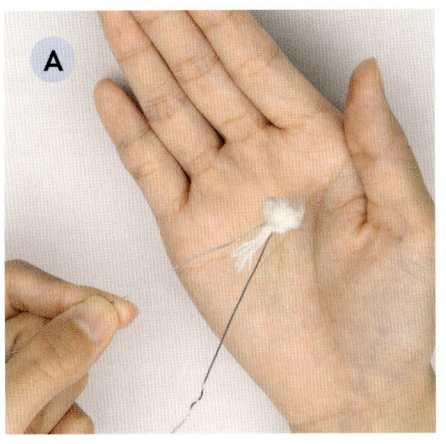
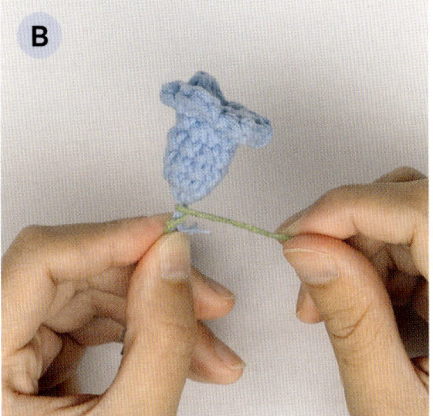

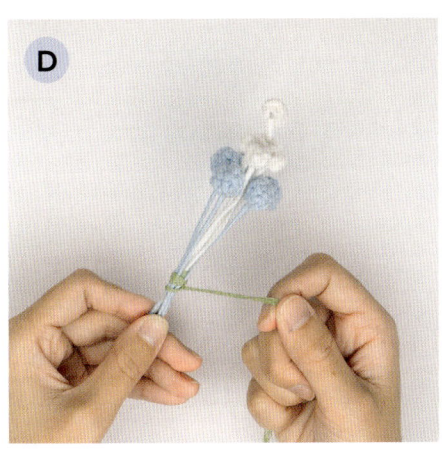

Assembly

1. Insert floral wire into the bases of the small buds, fold, and twist to secure (A). Wrap yarn around from base to 6cm (2½in) length. Cut yarn. Repeat for medium buds and flowers (B).

2. Fix the first small white bud at the top of the stem and wrap it with green yarn. Continue fixing each layer of buds and flowers in sequence, wrapping each layer with green yarn to secure them to the stem (C, D, E).

The order to add the buds and flowers to the stem is as follows:

First layer: one small bud
Second layer: four small buds
Third layer: five medium buds
Fourth layer: six medium buds
Fifth layer: six flowers
Sixth layer: seven flowers

3. Begin wrapping green yarn around the stem, starting below the flowers. Add two leaves around 3cm (1¼in) down, attaching them to the stem with green yarn (F).

4. Wrap the yarn to the end of the stem and secure it with glue.

Peony

YARN

Cotton or cotton blend, 5-ply in white (10g / ½oz), pink (6g / ¼oz), dark pink (6g / ¼oz), green (10g / ½oz), yellow (3g / ¼oz)

HOOK

2mm (US 4)

MATERIALS

0.5mm floral wire for leaf: 1 x 30cm (12in) length

3mm floral stem: 1 x 40cm (16in) length

Fiberfill stuffing

Hot glue gun

PATTERN NOTE:

This pattern uses the amigurumi method of working in a spiral. Join each round with a slst into the top of the first sc. It will help to use a stitch marker in the first stitch of the round, so that you know when you have completed the round. Move the marker up as you work.

STAMEN

(MAKE 1)

Using yellow, make a magic ring.

Rnd 1 (RS): 1 ch (does not count as a st throughout), 8 sc into ring, join. (8 sts)

Rnd 2: 1 ch, [2 sc BLO in next st] 8 times, join. (16 sts)

Rnd 3: 1 ch, [1 sc BLO, 2 sc BLO in next st] 8 times, join. (24 sts)

You will now work two layers of stamen into the unused FLO of Rnds 2 and 1. The positions of the two layers are staggered.

First layer of stamen: Working into the FLO of Rnd 2, * [1 slst, 8 ch, 1 slst] in next st, skip 1 st; repeat from * 7 more times (A).

Second layer of stamen: Working into the FLO of Rnd 1, [1 slst, 8 ch] 8 times, slst.

Fasten off, weave in the end.

Change to green and continue working into Rnd 3 (B).

Rnds 4–6: 1 ch, 24 sc, join. (24 sts)

Rnd 7: 1 ch, [2 sc, 1 sc2tog] 6 times, join. (18 sts)

Rnd 8: 1 ch, 18 sc, join.

Rnd 9: 1 ch, [1 sc, 1 sc2tog] 6 times, join. (12 sts).

Add stuffing.

Rnd 10: 6 sc2tog, join. (6 sts)

Fasten off (C).

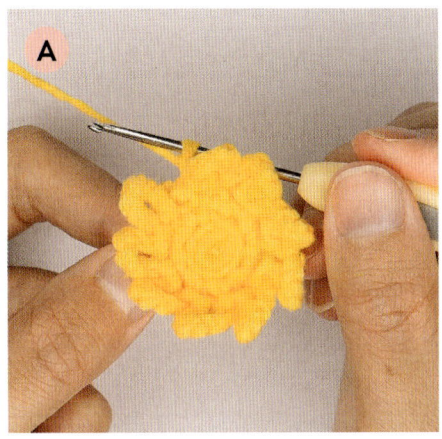
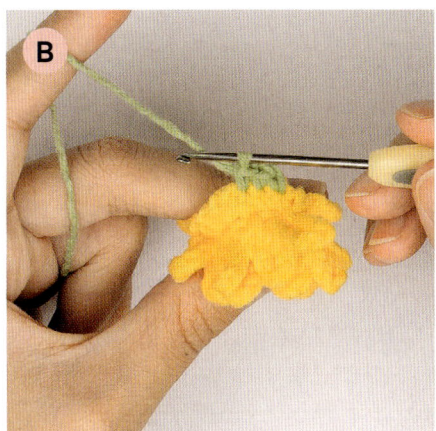
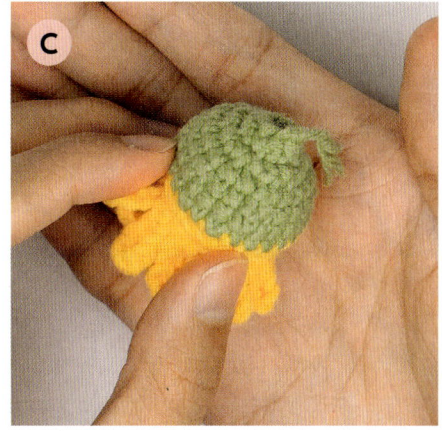

FIRST LAYER OF PETALS

Change to dark pink. Join yarn at the junction of Rnds 3 and 4 of stamen.

Now work in rows.

Row 1: 4 sc, turn. (4 sts)

Row 2: 3 ch (does not count as a st throughout), 4 tr, turn (4 sts)

Row 3: 2 ch (does not count as a st throughout), 1 dc, [2 dc in the next st] twice, [1 dc, 2 ch, 1 sc] all into the next st, 2 ch, 1 sc in the row end of Row 1. The first petal is complete (D).

Repeat Rows 1–3 another 5 times to make 6 petals in total (D).

Fasten off and weave in the end.

LACE OF PETALS

Join dark pink in the row end of the first st of Row 1 of first petal. You will be working around the edges of the petals.

Row 1: * 1 ch, 1 sc in sp between Row 1 and Row 2, 1 sc in row end of Row 2, [1 sc, 3 ch, 1 sc] in the first st of Row 3, [1 sc, 3 ch, 1 sc] in next st, skip 1 st, [1 sc, 3 ch, 1 sc] in next st, skip 1 st, [1 sc, 3 ch, 1 sc in next st], 1 sc in Row end of Row 2, 1 sc in sp between Row 1 and Row 2, 1 slst in the first sc of next petal; repeat from * 5 more times (E).

Fasten off and weave in the end.

SECOND LAYER OF PETALS

Change to pink. Join yarn at the junction of Rnds 4 and 5 of stamen.

Row 1: 4 sc, turn. (4 sts)

Row 2: 3 ch, 3 tr, 2 tr in the next st, turn. (5 sts)

Row 3: 2 ch, [1 dc, 2 dc in the next st] twice, [1 dc, 2 ch, 1 sc] all into the next st, 2 ch, 1 sc in the Row end of Row 1. The first petal is complete.

Repeat Rows 1–3 another 5 times to make 6 petals in total (F).

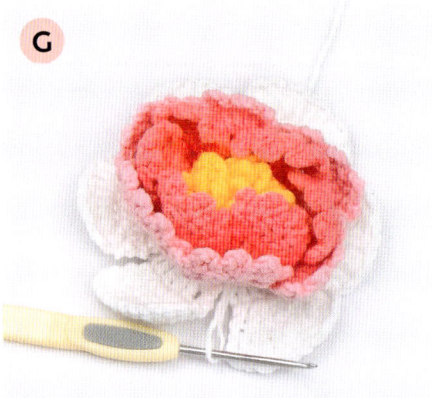
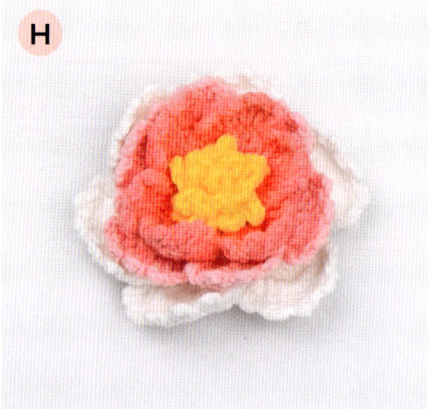

> ### Tip
> To make the petals look open and relaxed, crochet the edges with slightly looser stitches. If you'd like a contrasting finish, edge your peony with white yarn.

LACE OF PETALS

Join pink in the row end of the first st of Row 1 of first petal. You will be working around the edges of the petals.

Row 1: * 1 ch, 1 sc in sp between Row 1 and Row 2, 1 sc in Row end of Row 2, [1 sc, 3 ch, 1 sc] in the first st of Row 3, [1 sc, 3 ch, 1 sc] in next st, skip 1 st, [1 sc, 3 ch, 1 sc] in next st, skip 1 st, [1 sc, 3 ch, 1 sc] in next st, [1 sc, 3 ch, 1 sc] in next st, 1 sc in Row end of Row 3, 1 sc in sp between Row 2 and Row 1, 1 slst in the first sc of next petal; repeat from * 5 more times.

Fasten off and weave in the end.

THIRD LAYER OF PETALS

Change to white. Join yarn at the junction of Rnds 5 and 6 of stamen.

Row 1: 24 sc, turn. (24 sts)

Row 2: 3 ch, 3 tr, 2 tr in the next st, leave remaining sts unworked, turn. (5 sts)

Row 3: 2 ch, 1 dc, 2 dc in the next st, 1 dc, 2 dc in the next st, 1 dc, turn. (7 sts)

Row 4: 2 ch, [1 dc, 2 dc in the next st] 3 times, [1 dc, 2 ch, 1 sc] all into the next st, 2 ch, 1 sc in the Row end of Row 2, 1 sc in the Row end of Row 1. The first petal is complete.

Repeat Rows 2–4, 5 more times to make 6 petals in total (G).

Fasten off and weave in the end.

LACE OF PETALS

Join white in the row end of the first st of Row 1 of first petal. You will be working around the edges of the petals.

Row 1: * 1 ch, 1 sc in the Row end of Row 2, 1 sc in the Row end of Row 3, {[1 sc, 3 ch, 1 sc] all in the next st, skip 1 st} 4 times, {[1 sc, 3 ch, 1 sc] all in the next st} twice, 1 sc in the Row end of Row 3, 1 sc in sp between Row 3 and Row 2, 1 sc in the Row end of Row 2, 1 sc in sp between Row 2 and Row 1, 1 slst in the first sc of next petal; repeat from * 5 more times (H).

Fasten off and weave in the end.

LEAF

(MAKE 1)

Using green, ch 16.

Rnd 1: Starting in the 2nd ch from hook, working over floral wire, 1 sc, 1 hdc, 11 dc, 1 hdc, 2 sc in next ch, rotate to work into opposite side of ch, 1 hdc, 11 dc, 1 hdc, 1 sc, join. (30 sts)

Now work in rows.

Row 1: 1 ch, 1 sc, place marker in st just made, 1 hdc, 1 dc, 2 dc in the next st, [2 dc, 2 dc in the next st] twice, leave remaining sts unworked, turn. (13 sts)

Row 2: 1 ch, skip first st, 12 sc, turn. (12 sts)

Row 3: 1 ch, 1 sc, 1 hdc, 1 dc, 2 dc in the next st, 2 dc, 2 dc in the next st, 2 dc, leave remaining sts unworked, turn. (11 sts)

Row 4: 1 ch, skip first st, 10 sc, ** 1 ch (make this ch large), 1 slst in marked st on Row 1.

Now work the other side of the leaf:

Repeat Rows 1–4, ending Row 4 at **. Turn work to begin leaf lace (I).

LEAF LACE

Row 1: 1 ch, * [1 sc, 2 ch, 1 sc] in the next st, skip 1 st; repeat from * to end, working 1 sc and 1 slst at all corners (J).

Fasten off and weave in the end.

Assembly

1. Apply glue to the top of the floral stem and insert it into the flower base (K).

2. Wrap the floral stem with green yarn for 10cm (4in) (L). Add a leaf and secure it with yarn, wrapping until you reach the bottom (M). Apply glue to secure the end (N).

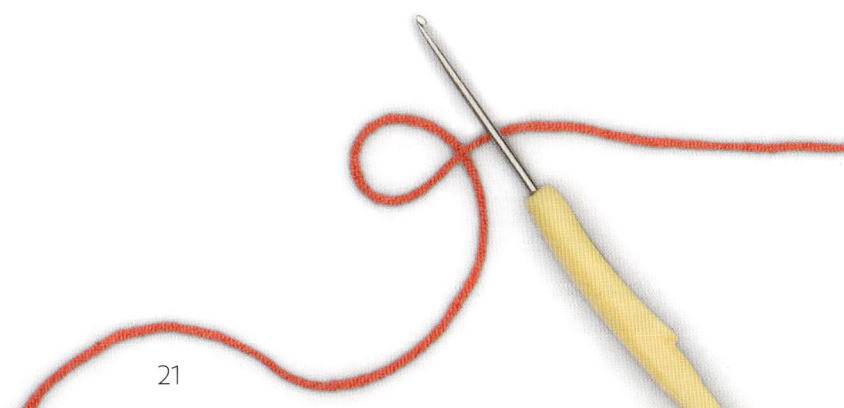

Sunflower

YARN

Cotton or cotton blend, 4-ply in yellow (10g / ½oz), green (20g / ¾oz), brown (5g / ¼oz), light brown (5g / ¼oz)

HOOK

2mm (US 4)

MATERIALS

0.6mm floral wire for leaf: 1 x 20cm (8in) length

3mm floral stem: 1 x 40cm (16in) length

Fiberfill stuffing

Hot glue gun

PATTERN NOTE:

This pattern uses the amigurumi method of working in a spiral. Join each round with a slst into the top of the first sc. It will help to use a stitch marker in the first stitch of the round, so that you know when you have completed the round. Move the marker up as you work.

FLOWER CENTER

(MAKE 1)

Using brown, make a magic ring.

Rnd 1: 1 ch (does not count as a st throughout), 6 sc into ring, join. (6 sts)

Rnd 2: 1 ch, [2 sc in the next st] 6 times, join. (12 sts)

Rnd 3: 1 ch, [1 sc, 2 sc in the next st] 6 times, join. (18 sts)

Rnd 4: 1 ch, [1 sc, 2 sc in the next st, 1 sc] 6 times, join. (24 sts)

Rnd 5: 1 ch, [3 sc, 2 sc in the next st] 6 times, join. (30 sts)

Rnd 6: Change to light brown. Working in FLO, [3ch-picot, skip 1 st] to end.

Rnd 7: Change to brown. 1 ch, working in BLO of Rnd 5, [4 sc, 2 sc in the next st] 6 times, join. (36 sts)

Rnd 8: Change to light brown. Working in FLO of Rnd 7, [3ch-picot, skip 1 st] to end.

Rnd 9: Change to brown. 1 ch, working in BLO of Rnd 7, [5 sc, 2 sc in the next st] 6 times, join. (42 sts)

Rnd 10: Change to light brown. Working in FLO of Rnd 9, [3ch-picot, skip 1] to end.

Rnd 11: Change to brown. 1 ch, working in BLO of Rnd 9, [6 sc, 2 sc in the next st] 6 times, join. (48 sts) (A)

Rnd 12: Change to light brown. Working in FLO of Rnd 11, [3ch-picot, skip 1] to end.

PETALS

(MAKE 16)

Using yellow, join in any st of Rnd 11 of flower center.

Rnd 1: * 8 ch, starting in the 2nd ch from hook, 7 sc, skip 1 st, 2 slst; repeat from * 15 more times (B).

Rnd 2: Working over floral wire, * working into opposite side of ch, 1 sc, 1 hdc, 3 dc, 1 hdc, 1 sc, [1 sc, 1ch-picot]

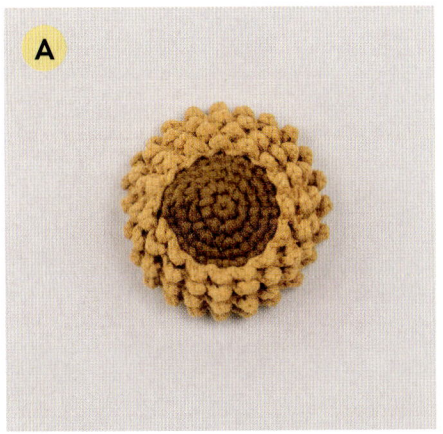
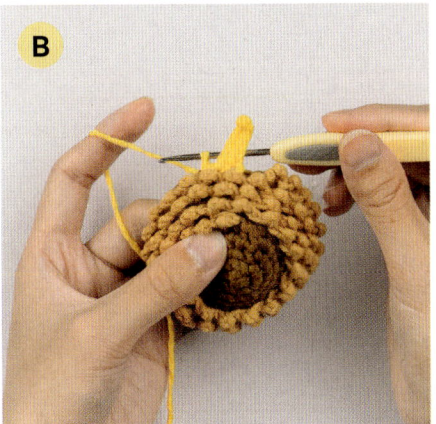

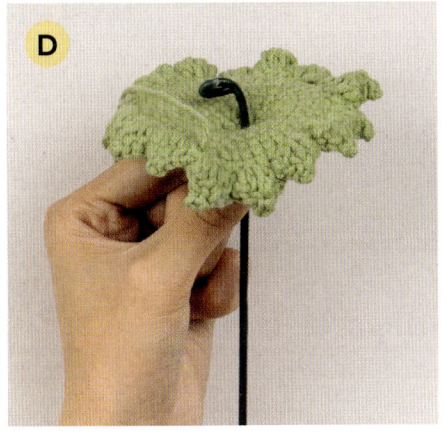

all into the next ch (at the tip of petal), working into the 7th sc of Row 1, 1 sc, 1 hdc, 3 dc, 1 hdc, 1 sc, skip 1 st, 1 slst; repeat from * 15 more times (C).

Fasten off and weave in the end.

CALYX
(MAKE 1)

Using green, make a magic ring.

Rnd 1: 1 ch, 6 sc into ring, join. (6 sts)

Rnds 2–3: 1 ch, 6 sc, join. (6 sts)

Rnd 4: 1 ch, [2 sc in the next st] 6 times, join. (12 sts)

Rnd 5: 1 ch, [1 sc, 2 sc in the next st] 6 times, join. (18 sts)

Rnd 6: 1 ch, [1 sc, 2 sc in the next st, 1 sc] 6 times, join. (24 sts)

Rnd 7: 1 ch, [3 sc, 2 sc in the next st] 6 times, join. (30 sts)

Rnd 8: 1 ch, [2 sc, 2 sc in the next st, 2 sc] 6 times, join. (36 sts)

Rnd 9: 1 ch, [5 sc, 2 sc in the next st] 6 times, join. (42 sts)

Rnd 10: 1 ch, [3 sc, 2 sc in the next st, 3 sc] 6 times, join. (48 sts)

Rnd 11: 1 ch, 48 sc, join. (48 sts)

Rnd 12: 1 ch, * [2 dc, 2ch-picot, 2 dc] all into the next st, 1 slst in the next st, skip 1 st; repeat from * 15 more times.

Fasten off and weave in the end.

LEAF
(MAKE 1)

Using green, make a magic ring.

Rnd 1: 1 ch, 7 sc into ring. (7 sts)

Rnd 2: 2 ch, 3 dc in the next st, [2 dc in the next st] twice, 3 tr in the next st, [2 dc in the next st] twice, 3 dc in the next st. (17 sts)

Rnd 3: 1 ch, working over floral wire, [1 sc, 1 hdc] all into the next st, 3 dc in the next st, [2 dc in the next st] 6 times, 3 tr in the next st, [2 dc in the next st] 6 times, 3 dc in the next st, [1 hdc, 1 sc] all into the next st. (37 sts)

Rnd 4: 1 ch, 1 sc, 1 hdc, [2 dc in the next st] 5 times, 11 dc, [1 dc, 1 tr, 2ch-picot, 1 tr, 1 dc] in the next st, 11 dc, [2 dc in the next st] 5 times, 1 hdc, 1 sc. (50 sts)

Fasten off and weave in the end.

Assembly

1. Bend the top of the floral stem with needle-nose pliers, apply glue, and insert it into the calyx (D).

2. Sew the flower base and flower center together, then stuff with fiberfill (E).

3. Wrap the floral stem with green yarn for about 5cm (2in) then add a leaf (F). Continue wrapping the yarn to the base and secure it with glue.

Lily

YARN

Cotton or cotton blend, 4-ply in white (15g / ¾oz), green (14g / ½oz), yellow (2g / ¼oz)

HOOK

2mm (US 4)

MATERIALS

0.5mm floral wire for leaves: 2 x 20cm (8in) lengths

2mm floral stem: 3 x 40cm (16in) lengths

0.5mm floral wire for petals: 6 x 30cm (12in) lengths

0.5mm floral wire for flower center: 5 x 10cm (4in) lengths

Fiberfill stuffing

Hot glue gun

PATTERN NOTE:

This pattern uses the amigurumi method of working in a spiral. Join each round with a slst into the top of the first sc. It will help to use a stitch marker in the first stitch of the round, so that you know when you have completed the round. Move the marker up as you work.

PETAL

(MAKE 6)

Using white, ch 25.

Rnd 1: Starting in the 2nd ch from hook, 2 sc, 2 hdc, 14 dc, 3 hdc, 2 sc, 3 sc in the next st, rotate to work into opposite side of ch, 2 sc, 3 hdc, 14 dc, 2 hdc, 2 sc, join. (49 sts)

Rnd 2: Working over floral wire, 1 ch (does not count as a st throughout), 2 sc in the next st, 2 sc, 2 hdc, 1 dc, 2 dc in the next st, 4 dc, 2 dc in the next st, 5 dc, 3 hdc, 4 sc, [1 sc, 2ch-picot, 1 sc] in the next st, 4 sc, 3 hdc, 5 dc, 2 dc in the next st, 4 dc, 2 dc in the next st, 1 dc, 2 hdc, 2 sc, 2 sc in the next st, join. (56 sts)

Fasten off and weave in the end.

LEAF

(MAKE 2)

Using green, ch 30.

Rnd 1: Starting in the 2nd ch from hook, 1 ch, 2 sc, 2 hdc, 20 dc, 2 hdc, 2 sc, 3 sc in the next st, rotate to work into opposite side of ch, 2 sc, 2 hdc, 20 dc, 2 hdc, 2 sc, join. (59 sts)

Rnd 2: Working over floral wire, 29 sc, [1 sc, 2ch-picot] in the next st, 29 sc, join. (59 sts)

Fasten off and weave in the end.

STAMEN

(MAKE 5)

Using yellow, ch 5.

Row 1: Starting in the 2nd ch from hook, 4 slst.

Fasten off.

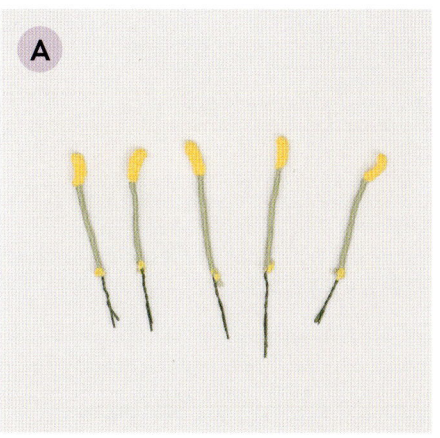
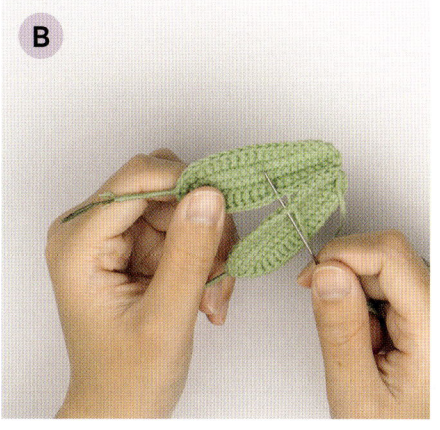
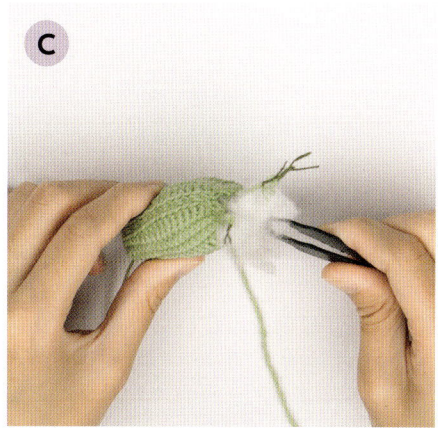
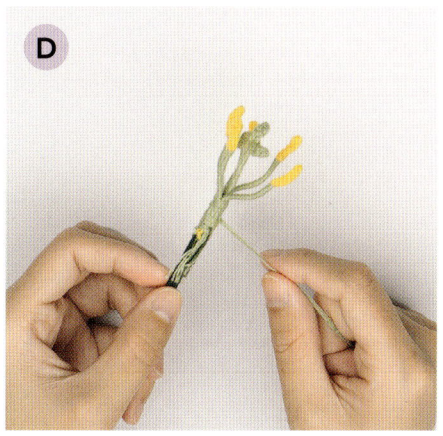

PISTIL

Using green, working into a magic ring, [4 ch, 3 slst] 3 times. Tighten ring.

Fasten off.

BUD SLICE

(MAKE 3)

Using green, ch 19.

Rnd 1: Starting in the 2nd ch from hook, working over floral wire, 17 sc, 3 sc in the next st, rotate to work into opposite side of ch, 17 sc, join. (37 sts)

Rnd 2: 1 ch, 1 sc, 1 hdc, 8 dc, 3 hdc, 5 sc, 2 sc in the next st, 5 sc, 3 hdc, 8 dc, 1 hdc, 1 sc, join. (38 sts)

Fasten off.

Assembly

1. Insert a 10cm (4in) piece of floral wire into the bottom of each stamen, fold in half, and wrap the wire with green yarn. Twist wire to secure the end (A).

2. Insert a 10cm (4in) piece of floral wire into the bottom of the pistil, fold in half, and wrap the wire with green yarn. Twist wire to secure the end.

3. Sew the three bud slices together, leaving an opening at the top (B). Stuff with fiberfill and shape into a bud (C).

4. Insert a stem into the bud, wrap with green yarn for 10cm (4in), add a leaf, and continue wrapping with green yarn for another 3cm (1¼in).

5. Take another stem, arrange five stamens around one pistil, and secure them at the top of the floral stem with green yarn (D).

6. Attach six petals sequentially to the stem, securing them with yarn, and shaping them into a lily flower (E).

7. Continue wrapping the floral stem for 5cm (2in), add another stem with a bud, wrap all stems together with yarn for 1cm (½in), add another leaf, and continue wrapping to the bottom (F). Secure the end with glue.

Common Rose

YARN
Cotton or cotton blend, 4-ply in pink (10g / ½oz) and green (6g / ¼oz)

HOOK
2mm (US 4)

MATERIALS
0.5mm floral wire for leaves: 3 x 15cm (6in) lengths

2mm floral stem: 1 x 40cm (16in) length

0.5mm floral wire for bud: 1 x 20cm (8in) length

Hot glue gun

PATTERN NOTE:
This pattern uses the amigurumi method of working in a spiral. Join each round with a slst into the top of the first sc. It will help to use a stitch marker in the first stitch of the round, so that you know when you have completed the round. Move the marker up as you work.

SMALL PETAL
(MAKE 4)

Using pink, make a magic ring.

Rnd 1 (RS): 1 ch (does not count as a st throughout), 8 dc into ring, join. (8 sts)

Rnd 2: 1 ch, [2 sc in the next st] 7 times, 1 sc, join. (15 sts)

Rnd 3: 1 ch, 2 sc, [1 sc, 1 ch] 11 times, 2 sc, join.

Fasten off and weave in the end.

MEDIUM PETAL
(MAKE 3)

Using pink, make a magic ring.

Rnd 1: 1 ch, 15 dc into ring, join. (15 sts)

Rnd 2: 1 ch, [2 sc, 2 sc in the next st] 5 times, join. (20 sts)

Rnd 3: 1 ch, 6 sc, [1 sc, 1 ch] 9 times, 5 sc, join. (20 sts)

Fasten off and weave in the end.

Tip
When wrapping the yarn around the flower stem, you can apply a small amount of glue to the stem. This will help keep the yarn from loosening.

LARGE PETAL
(MAKE 5)

Using pink, make a magic ring.

Rnd 1: 1 ch, 15 dc into ring, join. (15 sts)

Rnd 2: 1 ch, [2 dc in the next st] 6 times, [1 dc, 1 ch, 1 sc] all into the next st, [1 sc, 1 ch, 1 dc] all into the next st, [2 dc in the next st] 7 times, join. (30 sts)

Fasten off and weave in the end.

BUD
(MAKE 1)

Using pink, make a magic ring.

Rnd 1: 1 ch, 5 sc into ring, join. (5 sts)

Rnd 2: 1 ch, [2 sc in the next st] 5 times, join. (10 sts)

Rnds 3–7: 1 ch, 10 sc, join.

Rnd 8: 1 ch, [1 sc2tog] 5 times, join. (5 sts)

Fasten off and weave in the end.

FLOWER CALYX
(MAKE 1)

Using green, make a magic ring.

Rnd 1: 1 ch, 6 sc into ring, join. (6 sts)

Rnd 2: 1 ch, [2 sc in the next st] 6 times, join. (12 sts)

Rnd 3: 1 ch, [1 sc, 2 sc in the next st] 6 times, join. (18 sts)

Rnd 4: 1 ch, 18 sc, join. (18 sts)

Now work in rows.

Row 5: * 9 ch, starting in the 2nd ch from the hook, 2 slst, 1 sc, 2 hdc, 2 dc, 1 tr, skip 2 st, 1 slst ; repeat from * 5 more times, join.

Fasten off and weave in the end.

BUD CALYX
(MAKE 1)

Using green, make a magic ring.

Rnd 1: 1 ch, 5 sc into ring, join. (5 sts)

Rnd 2: 1 ch, [2 sc in the next st] 5 times, join. (10 sts)

Rnd 3: 1 ch, [4 sc, 2 sc in the next st] twice, join. (12 sts)

Rnd 4: 1 ch, 12 sc, join.

Rnd 5: 1 ch, * 7 ch, starting in the 2nd ch from the hook, 1 slst, 1 sc, 1 hdc, 2 dc, 1 tr, skip 2 sts, 1 slst; repeat from * 3 more times, join.

Fasten off and weave in the end.

LEAF
(MAKE 3)

Using green, ch 12.

Rnd 1: Starting in the 2nd ch from the hook, working over floral wire, 1 sc, 1 hdc, 1 dc, 4 tr, 1 dc, 1 hdc, 1 sc, 3 sc in the next st, 1 sc, 1 hdc, 1 dc, 4 tr, 1 dc, 1 hdc, 1 sc, join. (23 sts)

Rnd 2: 1 ch, [1 sc, 2 ch] 11 times, [1 sc, 2ch-picot, 1 sc] all into the next st, [2 ch, 1 sc] 11 times.

Fasten off and weave in the end.

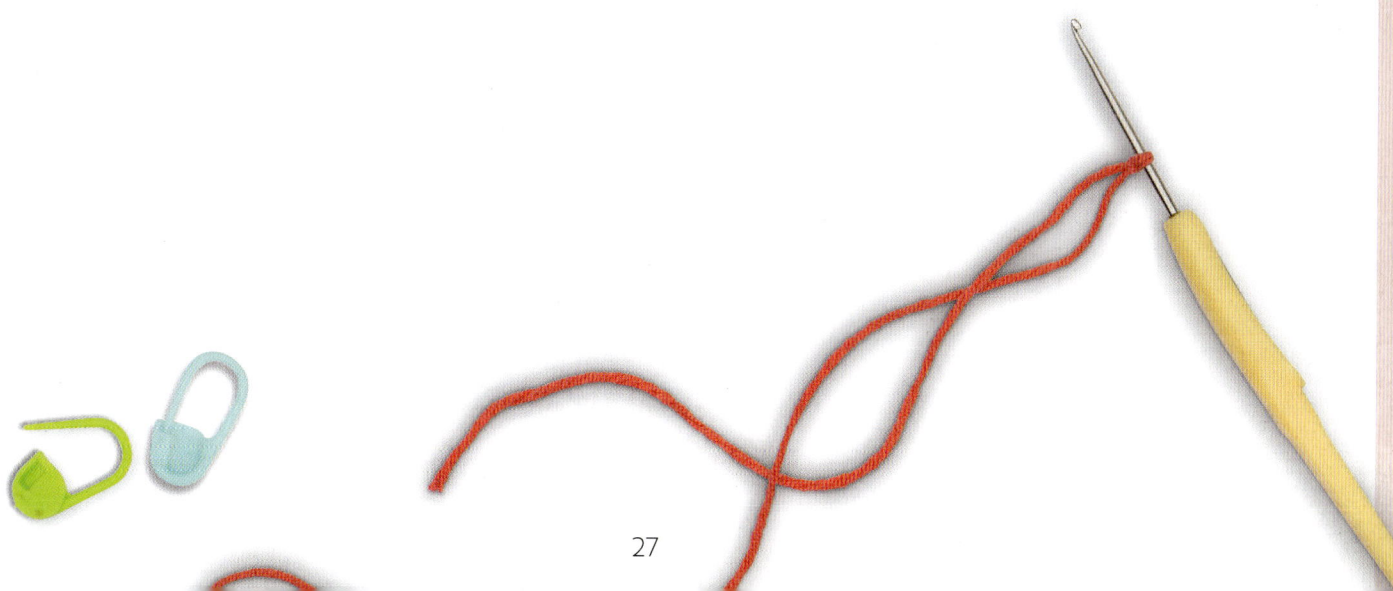

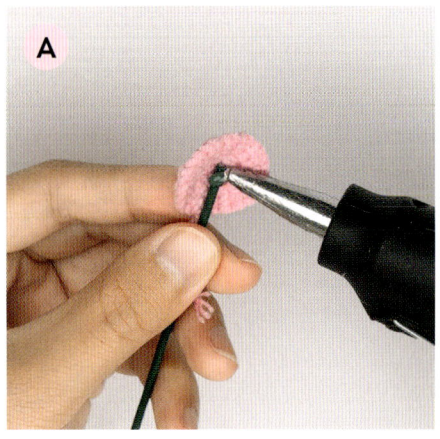 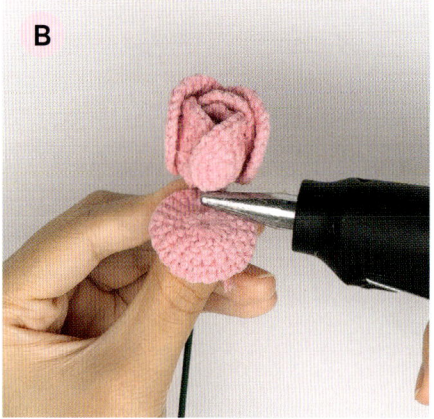 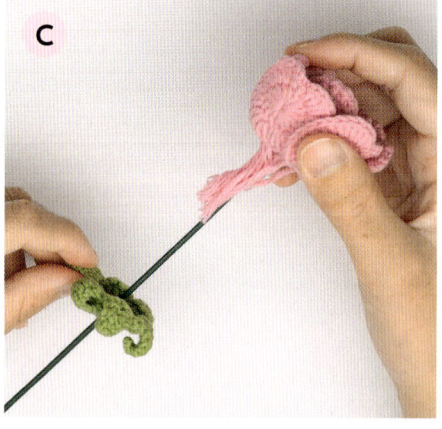

Assembly

1. Apply a small amount of hot glue to the top of the stem where it meets the petal base. To maintain the natural appearance of the petal, be careful not to use too much glue. Press the petal to the stem, ensuring the hot glue firmly holds it in place (A). Wait for the glue to completely dry and cool.

2. Gradually add more petals around the first petal and the stem center (B). Each new petal should slightly overlap the edge of the previous one to create a layered effect. Secure them all with hot glue.

3. Thread the flower calyx through the stem, positioning it at the base of the flower (C). Apply hot glue to secure it.

4. Gather the three leaves together (D).

5. Assemble the bud and calyx. Thread 20cm (8in) floral wire through the base of the bud and into the calyx (E). Push the calyx up to the bud. Wrap the wire with green yarn and twist to secure the yarn.

6. Wrap the floral stem with green yarn for 5cm (2in), add a bud and leaves, continue wrapping, and secure the end with glue (F).

Epiphyllum

YARN

Cotton or cotton blend, 4-ply in white (8g / ½oz), pink (10g / ½oz), light pink (10g / ½oz), dark pink (15g / ¾oz), green (8g / ½oz), yellow (2g / ¼oz)

HOOK
2mm (US 4)

MATERIALS

0.5mm floral wire for leaves: 2 x 15cm (6in) lengths

0.5mm floral wire to secure flower center

0.5mm floral wire for stamens: 8 x 30cm (12in) lengths

2mm floral stem: 2 x 40cm (16in) lengths

Hot glue gun

PATTERN NOTE:
This pattern uses the amigurumi method of working in a spiral. Join each round with a slst into the top of the first sc. It will help to use a stitch marker in the first stitch of the round, so that you know when you have completed the round. Move the marker up as you work.

FIRST-LAYER PETAL
(MAKE 6)

Using white, ch 17.

Rnd 1: Starting in the 2nd ch from hook, working over floral wire, 3 sc, 3 hdc, 4 dc, 2 tr, 2 dc, 1 hdc, 3 sc in the next st, rotate to work into opposite side of ch, 1 hdc, 2 dc, 2 tr, 4 dc, 3 hdc, 3 sc, join. (33 sts)

Fasten off and weave in the end.

SECOND-LAYER PETAL
(MAKE 8)

Using light pink, ch 20.

Rnd 1: Starting in the 2nd ch from hook, working over floral wire, 3 sc, 3 hdc, 5 dc, 3 tr, 2 dc, 2 hdc, 3 sc in the next st, rotate to work into opposite side of ch, 2 hdc, 2 dc, 3 tr, 5 dc, 3 hdc, 3 sc, join. (39 sts)

Fasten off and weave in the end.

THIRD-LAYER PETAL
(MAKE 8)

Using pink, ch 25.

Rnd 1: Starting in the 2nd ch from hook, working over floral wire, 11 sc, 3 hdc, 4 dc, 3 hdc, 2 sc, 3 sc in the next st, rotate to work into opposite side of ch, 2 sc, 3 hdc, 4 dc, 3 hdc, 11 sc, join. (49 sts)

Fasten off and weave in the end.

FOURTH-LAYER PETAL
(MAKE 8)

Using dark pink, ch 25.

Rnd 1: Starting in the 2nd ch from hook, working over floral wire, 24 sc, [1 sc, 3ch-picot, 1 sc] all into the next st, rotate to work into opposite side of ch, 24 sc, join. (50 sts)

Fasten off and weave in the end.

LEAF
(MAKE 2)

Using green, ch 29.

Rnd 1: Starting in the 2nd ch from hook, 27 sc, 3 sc in the next st, rotate to work into opposite side of ch, 27 sc, join. (57 sts)

Rnd 2: Working over floral wire, 1 ch (does not count as a st throughout), [1 sc, 1 hdc, 1 dc, 1 tr, 2 tr in the next st, 3 ch, 1 slst] 4 times, 1 sc, 1 hdc, 1 dc, [1 dc, 1 hdc] all into the next st, 3 sc in the next st, [1 dc, 1 hdc] all into the next st, 1 dc, 1 hdc, 1 sc, [1 sc, 1 hdc, 1 dc, 1 tr, 2 tr in the next st, 3 ch, 1 slst] 4 times.

Fasten off and weave in the end.

Assembly

1. To make the flower center, wrap yellow yarn around four fingers 10 times (A). Slip the loops off your fingers, then wrap a wire around the center of the loops and fold it in half (B). Cut the yarn loops at the ends (C) and trim the strands to shape them into the flower center (D).

2. Apply glue to the top of the floral stem and secure the flower center at the top.

3. Place the first layer of small petals closely around the flower center and secure them with green yarn (E).

4. Add the second layer of petals, slightly offsetting them from the first layer, and secure with green yarn (F).

5. Using the same method, continue adding the third and fourth layers of petals, ensuring each layer is offset from the previous one (G, H).

6. To make the stamen, wrap dark pink around the middle of a 30cm (12in) piece of floral wire for approximately 1cm (½in), then fold the wire in half (I). Continue wrapping the yarn around the entire length of the wire, ensuring a loop forms at the top. Repeat to make eight stamens (J).

7. Add the flower stamens in the last layer and secure them with yarn (K).

8. Wrap the stem with green yarn for about 10cm (4in), then add two leaves and secure them with yarn (L). Wrap down to the base of the floral stem and apply glue to fix the yarn in place.

> ### Tip
> *This method for creating a flower center can also be applied to other flowers, such as Lantern Lilies and Lily of the Valley.*

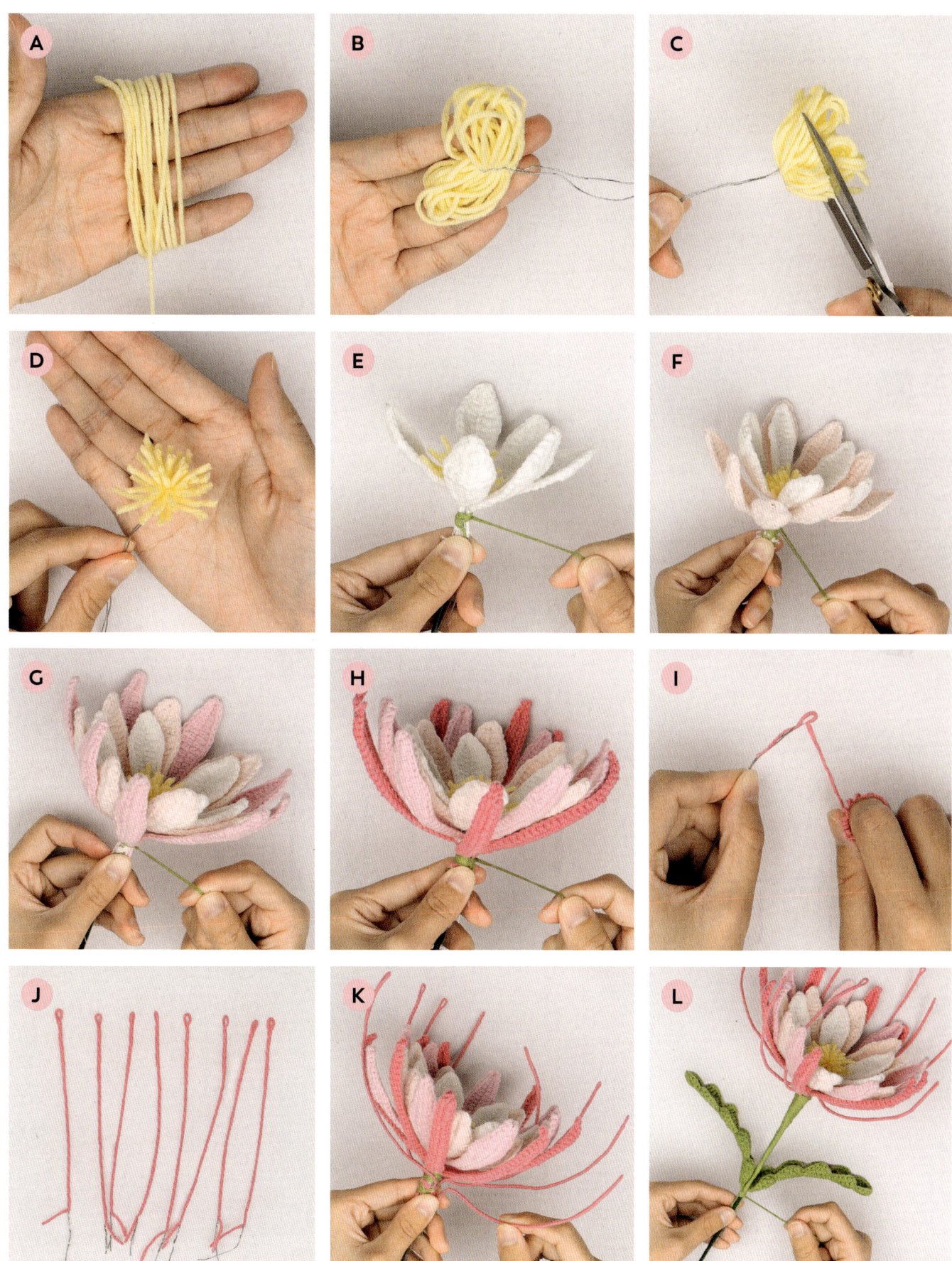

SECONDARY FLOWERS

These varieties support the main flowers, adding depth to an arrangement and complementing the focal blooms without overpowering them. They are typically smaller or less dramatic than the central flowers but still add balance, texture, and significant visual interest.

Tulip

YARN

Cotton or cotton blend, 5-ply in deep pink (15g / ¾oz), green (10g / ½oz), yellow (3g / ¼oz)

HOOK

2mm (US 4)

MATERIALS

0.5mm floral wire for leaf: 1 x 20cm (8in) length

0.5mm floral wire for petals: 6 x 20cm (8in) lengths

2mm floral stem: 1 x 40cm (16in) length

Hot glue gun

PATTERN NOTE:
This pattern uses the amigurumi method of working in a spiral. Join each round with a slst into the top of the first sc. It will help to use a stitch marker in the first stitch of the round, so that you know when you have completed the round. Move the marker up as you work.

SMALL PETAL
(MAKE 3)

Using deep pink, ch 13.

Rnd 1: Starting in the 2nd ch from hook, working over floral wire, 1 sc, 1 hdc, 7 dc, 1 hdc, 1 sc, 3 sc in the next st, rotate to work into opposite side of ch, 1 sc, 1 hdc, 7 dc, 1 hdc, 1 sc, join. (25 sts)

Rnd 2: 1 ch (does not count as a st throughout), 12 sc, 3 sc in the next st, 12 sc, join. (27 sts)

Fasten off, wrap yarn around the wire to secure and cut off the yarn.

BIG PETAL
(MAKE 3)

Using deep pink, ch 15.

Rnd 1: Starting in the 2nd ch from hook, 1 sc, 1 hdc, 9 dc, 1 hdc, 1 sc, 3 sc in the next st, rotate to work into opposite side of ch, 1 sc, 1 hdc, 9 dc, 1 hdc, 1 sc, join. (29 sts)

Rnd 2: Working over floral wire, 1 ch, 14 hdc, 3 sc in the next st, 14 hdc, join. (31 sts)

Fasten off, wrap the yarn around the wire to secure and cut off the yarn.

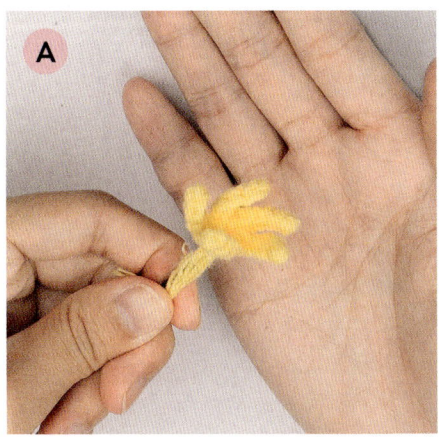

Tip
In nature, Tulips come in a rainbow of colors, from fresh white to dramatic purple. That means you can use almost any shade and your flower will still be realistic.

FLOWER CENTER
(MAKE 1)

Using yellow, make a magic ring.

Rnd 1: * 6 ch, don't tighten ring, starting in the 2nd ch from hook, 5 slst, 1 slst into ring; repeat from * 4 more times.

Tighten ring and fasten off.

LEAF
(MAKE 1)

Using green, ch 25.

Rnd 1: Starting in the 2nd ch from hook, working over floral wire, 2 sc, 3 hdc, 13 dc, 3 hdc, 2 sc, [1 sc, 3ch-picot, 1 sc] all into the next st, 2 sc, 3 hdc, 13 dc, 3 hdc, 2 sc, join. (48 sts)

Fasten off, wrap the yarn around the wire to secure and cut off the yarn.

Assembly

1. Fix the flower center on top of the stem and secure it with glue (A).

2. Place three small petals and three large petals around the flower center, ensuring they are staggered, then wrap the yarn to secure them (B, C).

3. Wrap the floral stem with green yarn for 5cm (2in), add a leaf, continue wrapping, and secure the end with glue (D).

Freesia

YARN

Cotton or cotton blend, 4-ply in white (10g / ½oz) and green (6g / ¼oz)

HOOK

2mm (US 4)

MATERIALS

0.6mm floral wire for leaf: 1 x 20cm (8in) length

0.6mm floral wire for buds: 2 x 10cm (4in) lengths

2mm floral stem: 1 x 40cm (16in) length

0.5mm floral wire for flowers: 5 x 15cm (6in) lengths

Hot glue gun

BIG FLOWER

(MAKE 1)

Using white, ch 4.

Row 1: Starting in the 4th ch from hook, 3 dc in next ch, turn. (3 sts)

Row 2: 3 ch (does not count as a st throughout), [3 dc in the next st] 3 times, turn. (9 sts)

Row 3: 3 ch, [2 dc in the next st] 9 times, turn. (18 sts)

Row 4: 4 ch, 1 tr in the first st, 2 tr in the next st, 3ch-picot, 1 tr, [1 tr, 4 ch, 1 slst] all into the next st, * [1 slst, 4 ch, 1 tr] all into the next st, [2 tr, 3ch-picot] all into the next st, [1 tr, 4 ch, 1 slst] all into the next st; repeat from * once more, 2 slst, ** [1 slst, 4 ch, 2 tr, 3ch-picot] all into the next st, [1 tr, 4 ch, 1 slst] all into the next st; repeat from * twice more.

Fasten off and weave in the end.

MEDIUM FLOWER

(MAKE 3)

Using white, ch 4.

Row 1: Starting in the 4th ch from hook, 3 dc in the next ch, turn. (3 sts)

Row 2: 3 ch, [3 dc in the next st] 3 times, turn. (9 sts)

Row 3: 3 ch, [2 dc in the next st] 9 times, turn. (18 sts)

Row 4: [2 ch, 1 dc] in the first st, [2 dc, 3ch-picot] in next st, 1 dc, [1 dc, 2 ch, 1 slst] all into the next st, * [1 slst, 2 ch, 1 dc] all into the next st, [2 dc, 3ch-picot, 1 dc] all into the next st, [1 dc, 2 ch, 1 slst] all into the next st; repeat from * once more, 2 slst, ** [1 slst, 2 ch, 2 dc, 3ch-picot] all into the next st, [1 dc, 2 ch, 1 slst] all into the next st; repeat from * twice more.

Fasten off and weave in the end.

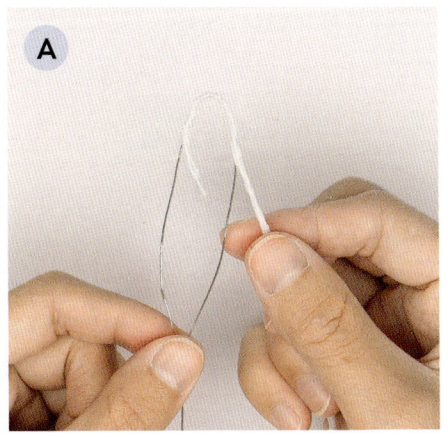
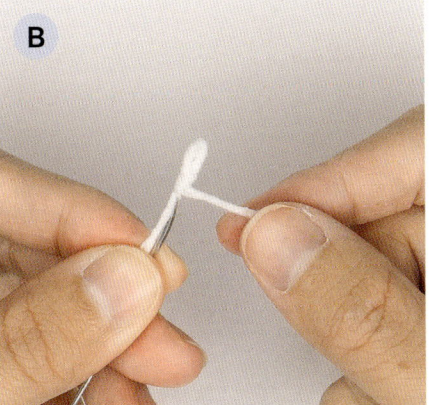

> **Tip**
> You can use this simple and effective method of making a small bud for many types of flower, including the Plum Blossom.

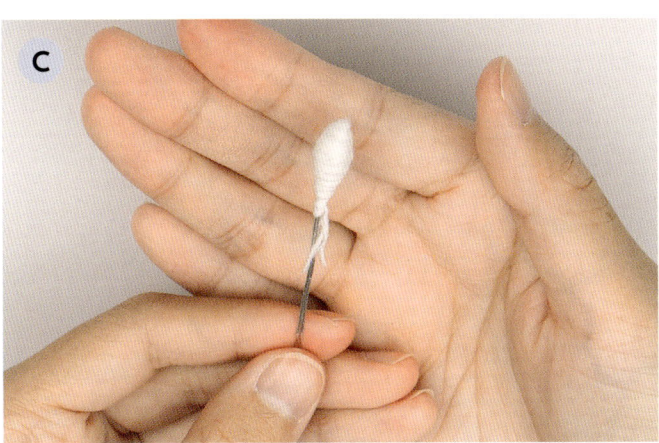

SMALL FLOWER
(MAKE 1)

Using white, ch 4.

Row 1: Starting in the 4th ch from hook, 3 dc in the next ch, turn. (3 sts)

Row 2: 3 ch, [3 dc in the next st] 3 times, turn. (9 sts)

Row 3: [2 ch, 1 dc] all into the first st, [1 dc, 3ch-picot] all into the next st, [1 dc, 2 ch, 1 slst] all into the next st, [2 ch, 1 dc] all into the next st, [1 dc, 3ch-picot] all into the next st, [1 dc, 2 ch, 1 slst] all into the next st, [1 slst, 2 ch, 2 dc, 3ch-picot] all into the next st, [1 dc, 2 ch] all into the next st, 1 slst in next st.

Fasten off and weave in the end.

LEAF
(MAKE 1)

Using green, ch 30.

Rnd 1: Starting in the 2nd ch from hook, working over floral wire, 1 slst, 3 sc, 21 hdc, 3 sc, slst.

Fasten off and weave in the end.

CALYX
(MAKE 5)

Using green, make a magic ring.

Row 1: Working into ring, [2 ch, 1 dc, 3 ch, 1 slst] twice. Tighten ring.

Fasten off and weave in the end.

Assembly

1. To make a bud, wrap 1cm (½in) of the middle of a 10cm (4in) length of wire with 2-ply white yarn (A). Fold the wire in half and continue wrapping with white yarn to form a bud shape, thicker in the middle, and tapering at the ends (B, C). Wrap the lower half of the bud with green yarn down to the end of the wire (D). Repeat to make a second bud.

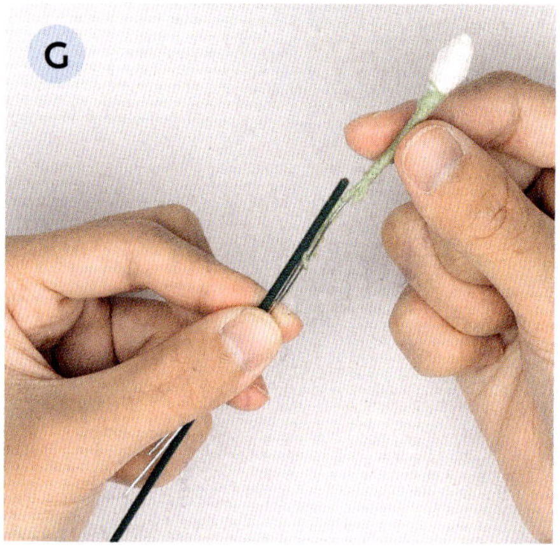

2. Roll up each of the flowers and secure with glue. Insert a 15cm (6in) wire into the base of the flower and fold it in half. Insert the wire through the calyx and use glue to secure the calyx to the base of the flower (E, F).

3. Attach two small buds to the top of the floral stem and secure them with green yarn (G). Continue wrapping the stem. At 1cm (½in) intervals, add the small flower, the medium flowers, and the large flower, securing each with yarn as you go (H, I).

4. Continue wrapping the stem to 5cm (2in) below the last flower, add a leaf, secure with yarn, and fix the end of the stem with glue (J).

Chinese Lantern Lily

YARN

Cotton or cotton blend, 4-ply in orange (18g / ¾oz), green (12g / ½oz), light green (5g / ¼oz), yellow (2g / ¼oz)

HOOK

2mm (US 4)

MATERIALS

0.5mm floral wire for leaves: 7 x 20cm (8in) lengths

2mm floral stem: 1 x 40cm (16in) length

0.5mm floral wire for flowers: 3 x 10cm (4in) lengths

0.5mm floral wire for buds: 3 x 10cm (4in) lengths

Hot glue gun

PATTERN NOTE:

This pattern uses the amigurumi method of working in a spiral. Join each round with a slst into the top of the first sc. It will help to use a stitch marker in the first stitch of the round, so that you know when you have completed the round. Move the marker up as you work.

FLOWER

(MAKE 3)

Using orange, ch 16, join with a slst in first st to form a ring.

Rnd 1: Work into FLO of ch, 1 sc in every ch around, join. (16 sts)

Rnd 2: 1 ch (does not count as a st throughout), 16 sc, join.

Rnd 3: 1 ch, [1 sc, 2 sc in the next st] 8 times, join. (24 sts)

Rnd 4: 1 ch, [2 sc, 2 sc in the next st] 8 times, join. (32 sts)

Rnd 5: 1 ch, [3 sc, 2 sc in the next st] 8 times, join. (40 sts)

Rnds 6–8: 1 ch, 40 sc, join.

Rnd 9: 1 ch, [3 sc, 1 sc2tog] 8 times, join. (32 sts)

Rnd 10: 1 ch, [2 sc, 1 sc2tog] 8 times, join. (24 sts)

Rnd 11: 1 ch, [4 sc, 1 sc2tog] 4 times, join. (20 sts)

Rnd 12: 1 ch, [8 sc, 1 sc2tog] twice, join. (18 sts)

Rnds 13–14: 1 ch, 18 sc, join.

Rnd 15: 1 ch, * [1 sc, 2 ch, 1 sc] all into the next st, 2 slst; repeat from * 5 more times.

Fasten off.

Using orange, sew the base of the flower (Rnd 1) closed.

BUD
(MAKE 3)

Using light green, make a magic ring.

Rnd 1: 1 ch, 6 sc into ring, join. (6 sts)

Rnd 2: 1 ch, [2 sc, 2 sc in the next st] twice, join. (8 sts)

Rnd 3: 1 ch, [3 sc, 2 sc in the next st] twice, join. (10 sts)

Rnds 4–5: 1 ch, 10 sc, join.

Rnd 6: 1 ch, 2 sc, 1 sc2tog, 2 sc, 1 sc2tog, 2 sc, join. (8 sts)

Fasten off and weave in the end.

BIG LEAF
(MAKE 2)

Using green, ch 30.

Rnd 1: Starting in the 2nd ch from hook, working over floral wire, 1 sc, 1 hdc, 25 dc, 1 hdc, [1 sc, 2 ch, 1 sc] in the next st, rotate to work into opposite side of ch, 1 hdc, 25 dc, 1 hdc, 1 sc, join. (58 sts)

Fasten off and weave in the end.

MEDIUM LEAF
(MAKE 3)

Using green, ch 16.

Rnd 1: Starting in the 2nd ch from hook, working over floral wire, 1 sc, 1 hdc, 11 dc, 1 hdc, [1 sc, 2 ch, 1 sc] in the next st, rotate to work into opposite side of ch, 1 hdc, 11 dc, 1 hdc, 1 sc, join. (30 sts)

Fasten off and weave in the end.

SMALL LEAF
(MAKE 2)

Using green, ch 13.

Rnd 1: Starting in the 2nd ch from hook, working over floral wire, 1 sc, 1 hdc, 8 dc, 1 hdc, [1 sc, 2 ch, 1 sc] in the next st, rotate to work into opposite side of ch, 1 hdc, 8 dc, 1 hdc, 1 sc, join. (24 sts)

Fasten off and weave in the end.

> **Tip**
>
> Using wire to create the flower center makes it easy to form into the perfect shape. The method is also used for the Lily of the Valley center.

Assembly

1. To make a flower center, divide 4-ply yellow yarn into 2-ply. Wrap 2-ply yarn around a 10cm (4in) wire, fold it in half to form the stamen shape, and secure the base. Repeat to make three in total.

2. Insert a center into each flower and secure it with green yarn. Then insert a 10cm (4 in) wire into the base of each bud, fold it in half, and secure it with yarn (A).

3. Wrap and secure two small leaves with yarn at the top of the floral stem (B).

4. Continue wrapping. At 1cm (½in) intervals, add a bud and a medium leaf to both sides of the floral stem (C).

5. Continue adding the remaining buds, flowers, and leaves (D).

6. Wrap to the end of the stem, secure it with glue (E).

Daisy

YARN

Cotton or cotton blend, 5-ply in white (8g / ½oz), green (15g / ¾oz), yellow (5g / ¼oz)

HOOK

2mm (US 4)

MATERIALS

0.5mm floral wire for leaves: 2 x 20cm (8in) lengths

2mm floral stem: 1 x 40cm (16in) length

0.5mm floral wire for flowers: 3 x 10cm (4in) lengths

0.5mm floral wire for buds: 2 x 10cm (4in) lengths

Fiberfill stuffing

Hot glue gun

PATTERN NOTE:

This pattern uses the amigurumi method of working in a spiral. Join each round with a slst into the top of the first sc. It will help to use a stitch marker in the first stitch of the round, so that you know when you have completed the round. Move the marker up as you work.

FLOWER CENTER: YELLOW PART

(MAKE 3)

Using yellow, make a magic ring.

Rnd 1: 1 ch (does not count as a st throughout), 6 sc into ring, join. (6 sts)

Rnd 2: 1 ch, [2 sc in the next st] 6 times, join. (12 sts)

Rnd 3: 1 ch, 12 sc, join. (12 sts)

Fasten off and weave in the end.

FLOWER CENTER: GREEN PART

(MAKE 3)

Using green, work as for the flower center's yellow part.

FLOWER PETAL

Place a yellow center on top of a green center. Using white, crochet the petals along the edges through both layers to join the centers, adding some fiberfill as you go.

Rnd 4: 1 ch, 12 sc, join. (12 sts)

Now work in rows.

Row 5: * [3 ch, 1 dc, 3 ch, 1 slst] all into the next st; repeat from * 11 more times. (12 petals)

Fasten off and weave in the end.

 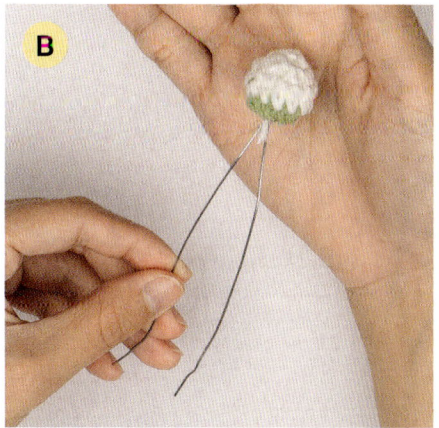 

BUD
(MAKE 2)

Using white, make a magic ring.

Rnd 1: 2 ch, 9 dc into ring, join. (9 sts)

Rnd 2: Change to green, 1 ch, 9 hdc, join. (9 sts)

Rnd 3: 1 ch, [1 sc, 1 sc2tog] 3 times, join. (6 sts)

Add some fiberfill.

Fasten off and weave in the end.

LEAF
(MAKE 2)

Using green, ch 14.

Rnd 1: Starting in the 2nd ch from hook, working over floral wire, 12 sc, 3 sc in the next st, rotate to work into opposite side of ch, 12 sc, join. (27 sts)

Rnd 2: 1 ch, [1 sc2tog, 2ch-picot, 1 slst in the next st] 9 times.

Fasten off and weave in the end.

Assembly

1. Insert a 10cm (4in) piece of floral wire into the bottom of each flower, fold in half. Wrap the wire with green yarn and twist the wire to secure the end (A).

2. Insert a 10cm (4in) piece of floral wire into the bottom of each bud and fold it in half (B). Wrap the wire with green yarn and twist the wire to secure the end.

3. Add the flower heads and buds sequentially to the floral stem at 1cm (½in) intervals. Secure each with yarn (C, D).

4. Add two leaves at 1cm (½in) intervals and secure with yarn (E). Apply glue at the base of the stem to fix everything in place (F).

Carnation

YARN

Cotton or cotton blend, 4-ply in light pink (5g / ¼oz), green (8g / ½oz), white (10g / ½oz)

HOOK

2mm (US 4)

MATERIALS

0.5mm floral wire for leaf: 1 x 20cm (8in) length

2mm floral stem: 1 x 40cm (16in) length

Fiberfill stuffing

Needle-nose pliers

Hot glue gun

PATTERN NOTE:

This pattern uses the amigurumi method of working in a spiral. Join each round with a slst into the top of the first sc. It will help to use a stitch marker in the first stitch of the round, so that you know when you have completed the round. Move the marker up as you work.

FLOWER
(MAKE 1)

Using white, make a magic ring.

Rnd 1: 3 ch (does not count as a st throughout), 12 dc into ring, join. (12 sts)

Rnds 2–4: 3 ch, 12 dc, join.

Rnd 5: 3 ch, [2 dc in the next st] 12 times, join. (24 sts)

Rnd 6: 3 ch, [3 dc in the next st] 24 times, join. (72 sts)

Rnd 7: 3 ch, [3 dc in the next st] 72 times, join. (216 sts)

Rnd 8: Change to pink, [3 ch, 1 sc] to end, join.

Fasten off and weave in the end.

CALYX
(MAKE 1)

With green, make a magic ring.

Rnd 1: 1 ch (does not count as a st throughout), 10 sc into ring, join. (10 sts)

Rnd 2: 1 ch, [1 sc, 2 sc in the next st] 5 times, join. (15 sts)

Rnds 3–11: 1 ch, 15 sc, join.

Rnd 12: * 3 ch, 1 dc2tog, 3ch-picot, 3 ch, 1 slst in the next st; repeat from * 4 more times.

Fasten off and weave in the end.

LEAF
(MAKE 1)

Using green, ch 25.

Rnd 1: Starting in the 2nd ch from hook, working over floral wire, 24 sc, 3 sc in the next st, rotate to work into opposite side of ch, 24 sc, join. (51 sts)

Fasten off and weave in the end.

Assembly

1. Use needle-nose pliers to bend the top of the floral stem and insert it through the flower (A, B).

2. Stuff an appropriate amount of fiberfill into the center of the flower head and sew it up tightly with thread (C, D).

3. Apply glue to the base of the flower head and insert it into the calyx to secure it (E).

4. Wrap the floral stem with green yarn for about 5cm (2in) and then add a leaf (F). Continue wrapping the yarn to the base and secure it with glue.

Lily of the Valley

YARN

Cotton or cotton blend, 4-ply in white (20g / ¾oz), green (15g / ¾oz), yellow (5g / ¼oz)

HOOK

2mm (US 4)

MATERIALS

0.6mm floral wire for leaves: 3 x 20cm (8in) lengths

2mm floral stem: 1 x 40cm (16in) length

0.5mm floral wire for flowers: 9 x 10cm (4in) lengths

Hot glue gun

PATTERN NOTE:

This pattern uses the amigurumi method of working in a spiral. Join each round with a slst into the top of the first sc. It will help to use a stitch marker in the first stitch of the round, so that you know when you have completed the round. Move the marker up as you work.

FLOWER
(MAKE 9)

Using white, make a magic ring.

Rnd 1: 1 ch (does not count as a st throughout), 6 sc into ring, join. (6 sts)

Rnd 2: 1 ch, [2 sc in the next st] 6 times, join. (12 sts)

Rnd 3: 1 ch, [2 sc in the next st] 12 times, join. (24 sts)

Rnds 4–7: 1 ch, 24 sc, join. (24 sts)

Rnd 8: 1 ch, [2 sc, 1 sc2tog] 6 times, join. (18 sts)

Rnd 9: 1 ch, * 1 sc, [1 dc, 1ch-picot, 1 dc] all into the next st, 1 sc; repeat from * 5 more times.

Fasten off and weave in the end.

LARGE LEAF
(MAKE 1)

Using green, ch 40.

Rnd 1: Starting in the 2nd ch from hook, 1 sc, 1 hdc, 34 dc, 1 hdc, 1 sc, 3 sc in the next st, rotate to work into opposite side of ch, 1 sc, 1 hdc, 34 dc, 1 hdc, 1 sc, join. (79 sts)

Rnd 2: Working over floral wire, 1 ch, 1 sc, 1 hdc, 35 dc, 1 hdc, 1 sc, [1 sc, 1ch-picot, 1 sc] all into the next st, 1 sc, 1 hdc, 35 dc, 1 hdc, 1 sc, join. (80 sts)

Fasten off and weave in the end.

MEDIUM LEAF
(MAKE 1)

Using green, ch 30.

Rnd 1: Starting in the 2nd ch from hook, 1 sc, 1 hdc, 24 dc, 1 hdc, 1 sc, 3 sc in the next st, rotate to work into opposite side of ch, 1 sc, 1 hdc, 24 dc, 1 hdc, 1 sc, join. (59 sts)

Rnd 2: Working over floral wire, 1 ch, 1 sc, 1 hdc, 25 dc, 1 hdc, 1 sc, [1 sc, 1ch-picot, 1 sc] all into the next st, 1 sc, 1 hdc, 25 dc, 1 hdc, 1 sc, join. (60 sts)

Fasten off and weave in the end.

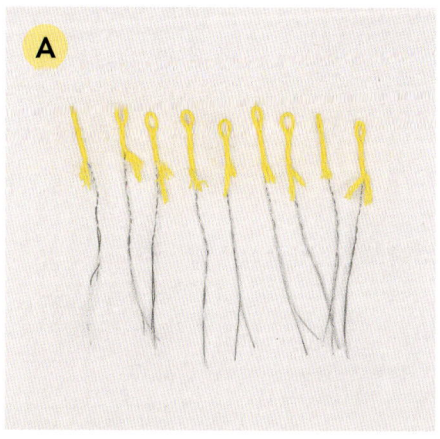

SMALL LEAF
(MAKE 1)

Using green, ch 25.

Rnd 1: Starting in the 2nd ch from hook, 1 sc, 1 hdc, 19 dc, 1 hdc, 1 sc, 3 sc in the next st, rotate to work into opposite side of ch, 1 sc, 1 hdc, 19 dc, 1 hdc, 1 sc. (49 sts)

Rnd 2: Working over floral wire, 1 sc, 1 hdc, 20 dc, 1 hdc, 1 sc, [1 sc, ch1-picot, 1 sc] in the next st, 1 sc, 1 hdc, 20 dc, 1 hdc, 1 sc, join. (50 sts)

Fasten off and weave in the end.

Assembly

1. To make the flower centers, split 4-ply yellow yarn into 2-ply. Wrap 2-ply around the middle of a piece of floral wire 10cm (4in) long. Fold the wire in half to form the stamen shape and twist to secure the base. Repeat to make nine in total (A).

2. Insert a flower center into each flower head and secure it by wrapping green yarn around the wire (B).

3. Attach nine flower heads sequentially to the floral stem and secure each with yarn. The first layer should have one flower, the second and third layers should have three flowers, and the fourth layer should have two flowers, with approximately 2cm (¾in) spacing between each layer (C, D).

4. Continue wrapping the stem for 5cm (2in). Add leaves, placing the large leaf in the center and the medium and small leaves on the sides, then secure with yarn (E).

5. Continue wrapping to the end, secure with glue (F).

Cosmos

YARN

Cotton or cotton blend, 4-ply in light pink (10g / ½oz), green (10g / ½oz), yellow (5g / ¼oz)

HOOK

2mm (US 4)

MATERIALS

0.6mm floral wire for leaf: 1 x 20cm (8in) length

2mm floral stem: 1 x 40cm (16in) length

Hot glue gun

PATTERN NOTE:

This pattern uses the amigurumi method of working in a spiral. Join each round with a slst into the top of the first sc. It will help to use a stitch marker in the first stitch of the round, so that you know when you have completed the round. Move the marker up as you work.

PETAL

(MAKE 8)

Using light pink, ch 7.

Rnd 1: Starting in the 2nd ch from hook, 2 sc, 1 hdc, 2 dc, 7 dc in the next st, rotate to work into opposite side of ch, 2 dc, 1 hdc, 2 sc, join. (17 sts)

Rnd 2: 4 ch, starting in the 2nd ch from hook, working over floral wire, 3 sc, [1 sc, 1 ch] 7 times, [1 sc, 2 ch, 1 sc] all into the next st 3 times, [1 ch, 1 sc] 7 times, 3 sc (into opposite side of beginning 4 ch), join. (26 sts)

Fasten off and weave in the end.

FLOWER CENTER

(MAKE 1)

Using yellow, make a magic ring.

Rnd 1: 1 ch (does not count as a st throughout), 5 sc into ring, join. (5 sts)

Rnd 2: 1 ch, [2 sc in the next st] 5 times, join. (10 sts)

Rnd 3: 1 ch, 10 sc, join. (10 sts)

Rnd 4: 1 ch, 5 sc2tog, join. (5 sts)

Fasten off and weave in the end.

LEAF

(MAKE 1)

Using green, ch 25.

Rnd 1: Starting in the 2nd ch from hook, working over floral wire, 23 sc, 3 sc in the next st, rotate to work into opposite side of ch, 23 sc, join. (49 sts)

Fasten off and weave in the end.

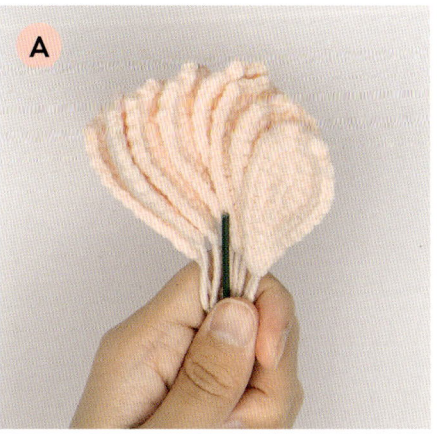
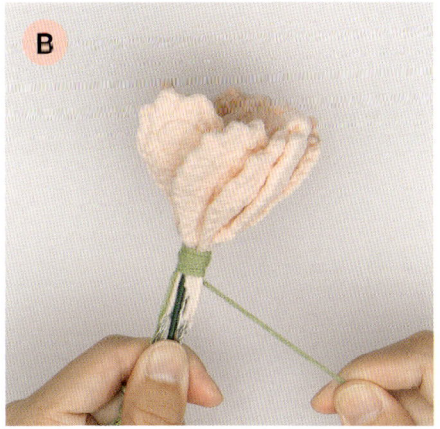

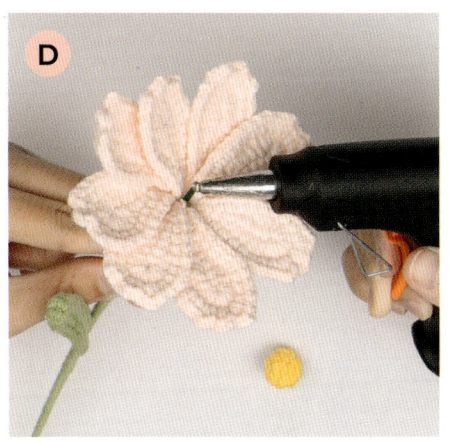

Assembly

1. Arrange all the petals evenly around the floral stem, overlapping them slightly, and secure them by wrapping with green yarn (A, B).

2. Wrap the floral stem with green yarn for about 5cm (2in), then add a leaf (C). Continue wrapping to the base and secure the yarn with glue.

3. Open out the petals, apply glue to the top of the stem, and attach the flower center (D, E).

Plum Blossom

YARN
Cotton or cotton blend, 4-ply in red (10g / ½oz) and brown (10g / ½oz)

HOOK
1.5mm (US 8/2)

MATERIALS
0.5mm floral wire for flowers: 5 x 10cm (4in) lengths

0.5mm floral wire for branch: 8 x 10cm (4in) lengths

2mm floral stem: 1 x 40cm (16in) length

0.5mm floral wire for buds: 5 x 15cm (6in) lengths

Artificial stamen

Hot glue gun

PATTERN NOTE:
This pattern uses the amigurumi method of working in a spiral. Join each round with a slst into the top of the first sc. It will help to use a stitch marker in the first stitch of the round, so that you know when you have completed the round. Move the marker up as you work.

SPECIAL STITCHES:
Bobble: [Yo, insert hook into next st or space as indicated, yo and pull a loop through, yo and pull through 2 loops] 4 times into same st or space, yo and pull through all 5 loops on hook.

FLOWER
(MAKE 5)

Using red, make a magic ring.

Rnd 1: 1 ch (does not count as a st throughout), 5 sc into ring, join. (5 sts)

Rnd 2: 1 ch, [2 sc in the next st] 5 times, join. (10 sts)

Rnd 3: 1 ch, 10 sc, join.

Rnd 4: 1 ch, [2 ch, 1 dc, 1 tr] all into the next st, [1 tr, 1 dc, 2 ch] all into the next st, * [1 slst, 2 ch, 1 dc, 1 tr] in the next st, [1 tr, 1 dc, 2 ch] all into the next st; repeat from * 4 more times.

Fasten off and weave in the end.

SMALL BUD
(MAKE 5)

Using red, make a magic ring.

Rnd 1: 2 ch, working into ring, 1 bobble, 1 ch, 1 bobble into 1ch-sp just made, tighten ring.

Fasten off.

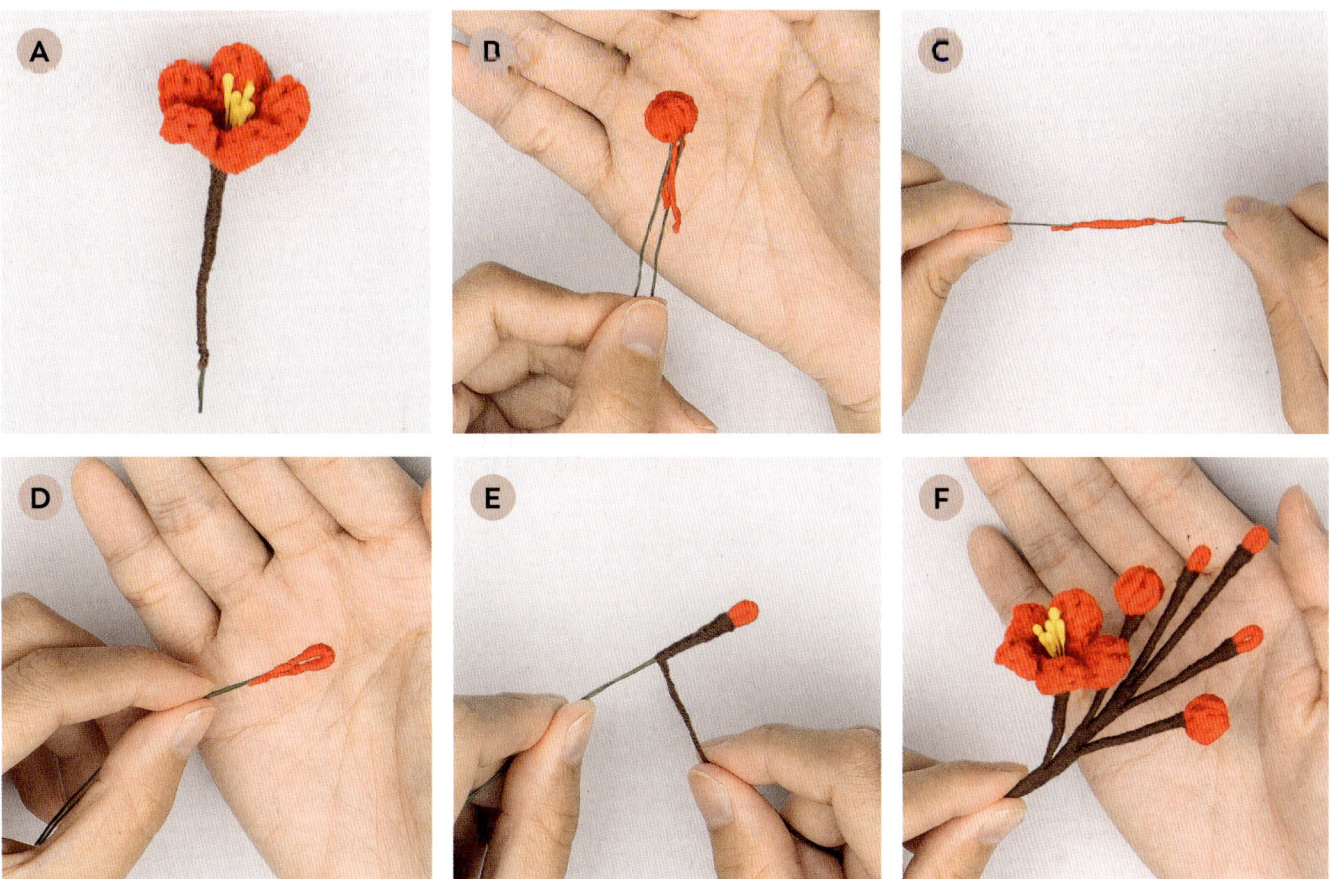

Assembly

1. Fix the artificial stamen in the middle of a piece of 10cm (4in) long floral wire. Fold the wire in half and insert it into the center of a flower. Wrap the wire with brown yarn and twist the wire to secure the end (A). Repeat for all flowers.

2. Fold the two bobbles of a bud together so that the chain space is at the center and the bobbles are on opposite sides. Insert a piece of 15cm (6in) long floral wire into the two bobbles and bend the wire into a U shape. Wrap the wire with brown yarn (B). Repeat for all buds.

3. To make a twig, wrap red yarn around the middle of a 10cm (4in) long piece of floral wire for about 1cm (½in) (C), then fold the wire in half (D). Continue wrapping brown around the entire length of the wire, ensuring a loop forms at the top (E). Repeat to make eight twigs.

4. Assemble the first side branch by combining three twigs, two buds, and one small flower (F).

> **Tip**
>
> *To achieve a natural effect that pleases your eye and completes a bouquet, you can assemble the flowers and buds in any way you like.*

5. Assemble the second side branch by combining three twigs, one bud, and one small flower (G).

6. Fix two twigs and one bud to the top of the floral stem, spaced 1cm (½in) apart. Wrap with thread to secure, then add another bud on the left of the stem, 2cm (¾in) lower. (H).

7. As you continue wrapping the yarn, place one flower on the right side of the stem with 1cm (½in) spacing. Add one flower on the left side, 2cm (¾in) lower, followed by another flower on the right side with a 1cm (½in) spacing (I).

8. With a 1cm (½in) spacing, add the second side branch on the right side of the stem, continue wrapping the yarn for 1cm (½in), and then add the first side branch on the left side (J).

9. Finally, add a small flower bud on the right side of the stem, wrap the yarn to secure the entire stem, and apply glue at the bottom of the stem to fix the end of the yarn (K).

Moth Orchid

YARN

Cotton or cotton blend, 4-ply in white (20g / ¾oz), green (5g / ¼oz), yellow (2g / ¼oz)

HOOK

1.5mm (US 8/7/2)

MATERIALS

0.5mm floral wire for front petals: 6 x 20cm (8in) lengths

0.5mm floral wire for back petals: 3 x 40cm (16in) lengths

0.5mm floral wire for buds: 2 x 15cm (6in) lengths

2mm floral stem: 1 x 40cm (16in) length

Fiberfill stuffing

Hot glue gun

PATTERN NOTE:

This pattern uses the amigurumi method of working in a spiral. Join each round with a slst into the top of the first sc. It will help to use a stitch marker in the first stitch of the round, so that you know when you have completed the round. Move the marker up as you work.

FRONT PETAL
(MAKE 6)

Using white, ch 13.

Rnd 1: Starting in the 2nd ch from hook, 2 sc, 8 hdc, 1 sc, 3 sc in the next st, rotate to work into opposite side of ch, 1 sc, 8 hdc, 2 sc, join. (25 sts)

Rnd 2: 1 ch (does not count as a st throughout), 3 sc, 1 hdc, 1 dc, 2 dc in the next st, 3 dc in the next st, 2 dc in the next st, 1 dc, 1 hdc, 2 sc, 3 sc in the next st, 2 sc, 1 hdc, 1 dc, 2 dc in the next st, 3 dc in the next st, 2 dc in the next st, 1 dc, 1 hdc, 3 sc, join. (35 sts)

Rnd 3: Working over a 20cm (8in) piece of floral wire, 17 sc, [1 sc, 1 ch, 1 sc] all into the same st, 1 sc in every st to end, join. (36 sts)

Fasten off and weave in the end.

BACK PETAL
(MAKE 3)

Using white, make a magic ring.

Rnd 1: * 12 ch, starting in the 2nd ch from hook, 11 sc, 1 slst into ring; repeat from * twice more, tighten ring, join. (33 sts)

Rnd 2: 1 ch, * working in opposite side of ch made in Rnd 1, 1 sc, 2 hdc, 1 dc, [2 dc in the next st] 3 times, 2 dc, 1 hdc, 1 sc, 3 sc in the next st, rotate to work into sts, 1 sc, 1 hdc, 2 dc, [2 dc in the next st] 3 times, 1 dc, 2 hdc, 1 sc; repeat from * 3 times, join. (93 sts)

Rnd 3: Working over 40cm (16in) piece of floral wire, 46 sc, [1 sc, 1 ch, 1 sc] all into the next st, 46 sc.

Fasten off and weave in the end.

SMALL PETAL
(MAKE 3)

Using white, ch 6.

Rnd 1: Starting in the 2nd ch from hook, 1 sc, [1 dc, 1 tr] all into the next st, 1 tr, [1 tr, 1 dc] all into the next st, 4 hdc in the next st, rotate to work into opposite side of ch, [1 dc, 1 tr] all into the next st, [1 tr, 1 dc] all into in the next st, 2 tr in the next st, [1 tr, 1 dc] all into the next st, [1 slst, 4 ch, 4 dtr, 4 ch, 1 slst, 4 dtr, 4 ch, 1 slst] all into the next st.

Fasten off and weave in the end.

FLOWER CENTER
(MAKE 3)

Using yellow, make a magic ring.

Rnd 1: Working into ring, [2 ch, 2 dc, 2 ch, 1 slst] twice. Tighten ring.

Fasten off and weave in the end.

BUD
(MAKE 1 GREEN AND 1 WHITE)

Make a magic ring.

Rnd 1: 1 ch, 6 sc into ring, join. (6 sts)

Rnd 2: 1 ch, [2 sc in the next st] 6 times, join. (12 sts)

Rnds 3–5: 1 ch, 12 sc, join. (12 sts)

Rnd 6: 1 ch, [1 sc, 1 sc2tog] 4 times, join. (8 sts)

Add some fiberfill.

Rnd 7: 1 ch, 4 sc2tog, join. (4 sts)

Fasten off and weave in the end.

Assembly

1. Place the two front petals onto the center of the back petals and secure with glue (A, B). Apply glue to the center of the front petals to attach the small petal (C). Finally, glue the yellow flower center onto the middle petal (D). Repeat to assemble all three flowers.

2. Insert a 15cm (6in) piece of floral wire into the bottom of each bud. Fold in half, wrap the wire with green yarn, and twist wire to secure the end (E).

3. Fix the white flower buds at the top of the stem and position the green bud 3cm (1¼in) lower down. Secure them with green yarn (F).

4. Continue wrapping the yarn for 3cm (1¼in), then fix the first flower on the stem (G). At 7cm (2¾in) intervals, add the second and third flowers (H).

5. Continue wrapping the yarn to the bottom of the stem, then secure the end with glue (I).

Tip

Feel free to increase or decrease the number and colors of the flowers and buds according to your preference. Don't hesitate to experiment!

Zephyr Lily

YARN

Cotton or cotton blend, 4-ply in white (25g / ¼oz), green (30g / 1oz), yellow (5g / ¼oz)

HOOK

2mm (US 4)

MATERIALS

0.5mm floral wire for leaves: 2 x 20cm (8in) lengths

0.5mm floral wire for flowers: 3 x 10cm (4in) lengths

0.5mm floral wire for flowers: 11 x 10cm (4in) lengths

0.5mm floral wire for twigs: 2 x 50cm (19¾in) lengths

2mm floral stem: 1 x 40cm (16in) length

Hot glue gun

PATTERN NOTE:

This pattern uses the amigurumi method of working in a spiral. Join each round with a slst into the top of the first sc. It will help to use a stitch marker in the first stitch of the round, so that you know when you have completed the round. Move the marker up as you work.

LARGE PETAL

(MAKE 12)

Using white, ch 20.

Rnd 1: Starting in the 2nd ch from hook, working over floral wire, 18 sc, 3 sc in the next st, rotate to work into opposite side of ch, 18 sc, join. (39 sts)

Rnd 2: 1 ch (does not count as a st throughout), 8 sc, 6 hdc, 2 sc, 3 slst, [1 sc, 1ch-picot, 1 sc] in the next st, 3 slst, 2 sc, 6 hdc, 8 sc, join. (40 sts)

Fasten off and weave in the end.

SMALL PETAL

(MAKE 5)

Using white, ch 15.

Rnd 1: Starting in the 2nd ch from hook, working over floral wire, 13 sc, 3 sc in the next st, rotate to work into opposite side of ch, 13 sc, join. (29 sts)

Rnd 2: 1 ch, 6 sc, 4 hdc, 2 sc, 2 slst, [1 sc, 1ch-picot, 1 sc] all into the next st, 2 slst, 2 sc, 4 hdc, 6 sc, join. (30 sts)

Fasten off and weave in the end.

LEAF

(MAKE 2)

Using green, ch 50.

Rnd 1: Starting in the 2nd ch from hook, working over floral wire, 48 sc, 3 sc in the next st, rotate to work into opposite side of ch, 48 sc, join. (99 sts)

Rnd 2: 49 slst, [1 sc, 1ch-picot, 1 sc] all into the next st, 49 slst, join.

Fasten off and weave in the end.

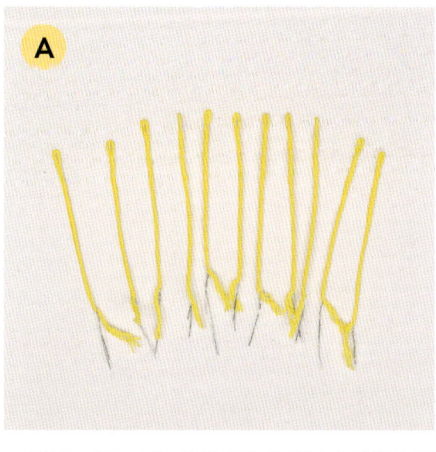 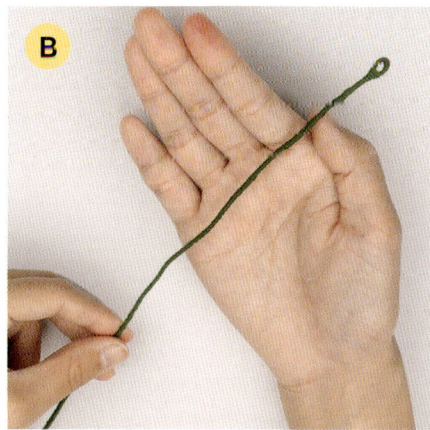 

Assembly

1. Split a 30cm (12in) length of 4-ply yellow yarn into 2-ply. Wrap 2-ply around a piece of 10cm (4in) long wire, fold it in half to form the stamen shape, and twist the wire to secure. Repeat to make eleven stamens (A).

2. To make a twig, wrap green yarn around the middle of a 50cm (19¾in) piece of wire for approximately 1cm (½in), then fold the wire in half. Continue wrapping the yarn down the entire length of the wire, ensuring a loop forms at the top (B). Repeat to make another twig.

3. Attach three stamens to the stem, wrap the yarn to secure them, and evenly distribute five small petals around the stamens, wrapping to secure (C). On another stem, attach four stamens to the top, evenly distribute six large petals around the stamens, and wrap to secure.

4. Wrap the stem of the small flower with green yarn for about 12cm (4¾in), add the large flower stem on the left side, continue wrapping for 2cm (¾in), and then add the twig on the right side (D).

5. Continue wrapping the stem for 2cm (¾in), add another large flower stem on the left side, continue wrapping for 1cm (½in), and then add another twig on the left side (E).

6. Continue wrapping the stem for 2cm (¾in), add one leaf on each side, and wrap the yarn down to the base of the stem, securing it with glue (F).

FILLER FLOWERS

Filler flowers are placed in the spaces between the main and secondary flowers to add texture and color. This makes the arrangement look fuller, lusher, and more polished. These blooms are usually smaller and can be quite delicate.

Winter Berry

YARN
Cotton or cotton blend, 4-ply in red (10g / ½oz) and brown (10g / ½oz)

HOOK
2mm (US 4)

MATERIALS
0.5mm floral wire for buds: 10 x 15cm (6in) lengths

2mm floral stem: 1 x 40cm (16in) length

Hot glue gun

SPECIAL STITCHES:
Bobble: [Yo, insert hook into next st or space as indicated, yo and pull a loop through, yo and pull through 2 loops] 4 times into same st or space, yo and pull through all 5 loops on hook.

BERRY
(MAKE 10)

Using red, make a magic ring.

Working into magic ring, 2 ch, 1 bobble, 1 ch, 1 bobble into 1ch-sp just made, tighten ring.

Fasten off.

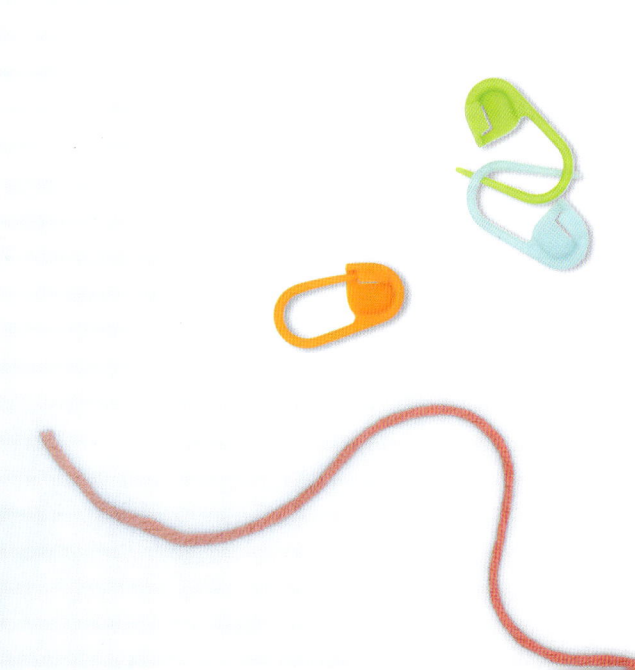

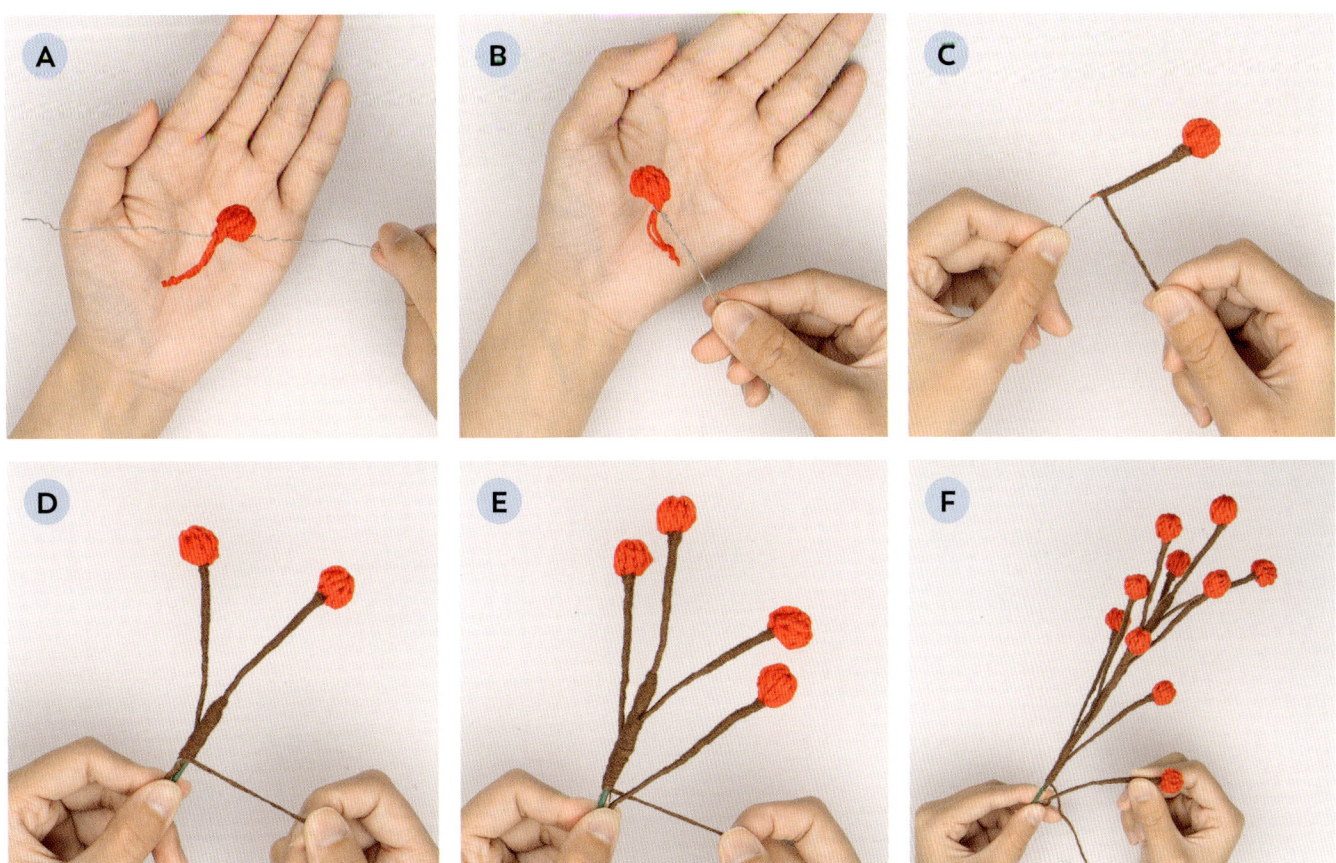

Assembly

1. Fold the two bobbles of a berry together so that the chain space is at the center and the bobbles are on opposite sides. Bend a 30cm (12in) length of floral wire around the base of the two bobbles (A), making a U shape (B). Wrap the wire with brown yarn to make a small twig (C).

2. Use brown yarn to attach 10 berries around the stem in all four directions at 1cm (½in) intervals, creating the effect of staggered height (D, E, F). Wrap yarn to the base of the stem and secure it with glue.

Spray Rose

YARN

Cotton or cotton blend, 4-ply in dark red (20g / ¾oz) and green (20g / ¾oz)

HOOK

2mm (US 4)

MATERIALS

0.5mm floral wire for leaves: 5 x 30cm (12in) lengths

0.5mm floral wire for flowers: 5 x 20cm (8in) lengths

3mm floral stem: 1 x 40cm (16in) length

Hot glue gun

PATTERN NOTE:

This pattern uses the amigurumi method of working in a spiral. Join each round with a slst into the top of the first sc. It will help to use a stitch marker in the first stitch of the round, so that you know when you have completed the round. Move the marker up as you work.

FLOWER

(MAKE 5)

Using dark red, ch 23.

Row 1: Starting in the 4th ch from hook, * 3 dc in the next st, 1 sc, skip 1 st; repeat from * 6 more times, 3 dc in the next st, 1 sc, turn. (32 sts)

Row 2: * 2 ch, 1 dc, 2 dc in the next st, 1 dc, 2 ch, 1 sc; repeat from * 6 more times (35 sts)

Fasten off and weave in the end.

LEAF

(MAKE 5)

Using green, ch 10.

Rnd 1: Starting in the 2nd ch from hook, working over floral wire, 1 sc, 1 hdc, 5 dc, 1 hdc, 3 sc in the next st, rotate to work into the other side of the ch, 1 hdc, 5 dc, 1 hdc, 1 sc, join. (19 sts)

Fasten off and weave in the end.

CALYX

(MAKE 5)

Using green, make a magic ring.

Rnd 1: 1 ch (does not count as a st throughout), 5 sc into ring, join. (5 sts)

Rnd 2: 1 ch, [2 sc in the next st] 5 times, join. (10 sts)

Rnd 3: * 5 ch, starting in the 2nd ch from hook, 2 slst, 1 sc, 1 hdc, skip 1 st, 1 slst; repeat from * 4 more times.

Fasten off and weave in the end.

Assembly

1. Apply glue to the inner base of the petals, then roll them to form the shape of the flower, securing them with glue to prevent them from unraveling (A).

2. Thread a 20cm (8in) wire through the base of the flower (B), fold the wire in half, and insert it into the center of the calyx. Secure the calyx at the base of the flower with glue, then wrap green yarn around the stem for about 5cm (2in) (C). Add a leaf and continue wrapping to secure it (D). Using the same method, assemble all five flowers.

3. Attach the five flowers to the top of the stem at varying heights (E, F), wrapping the stem in green yarn as you go. Wrap down to the bottom, then secure the end with glue.

Baby's Breath

YARN

Cotton or cotton blend, 4-ply in white (6g / ¼oz) and green (5g / ¼oz)

HOOK

2mm (US 4)

MATERIALS

0.5mm floral wire for flower centers: 6 x 20cm (8in) lengths

2mm floral stem: 1 x 40cm (16in) length

Pearl beads for flower centers

Hot glue gun

PATTERN NOTE:

This pattern uses the amigurumi method of working in a spiral. Join each round with a slst into the top of the first sc. It will help to use a stitch marker in the first stitch of the round, so that you know when you have completed the round. Move the marker up as you work.

FLOWER

(MAKE 6)

Using white, make a magic ring.

Rnds 1– 3: 1 ch (does not count as a st throughout), 5 sc, join. (5 sts)

Now work in rows.

Row 4: * 4 ch, starting in the 2nd ch from hook, 3 sc, 1 slst in next st; repeat from * 4 more times.

Fasten off and weave in the end.

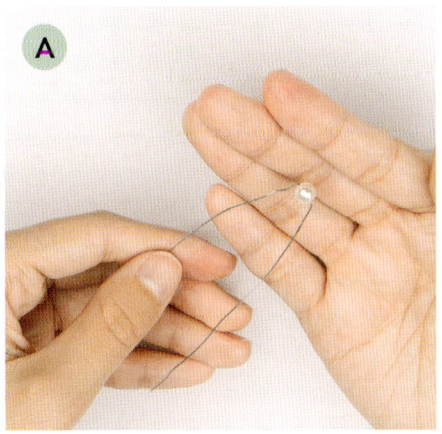
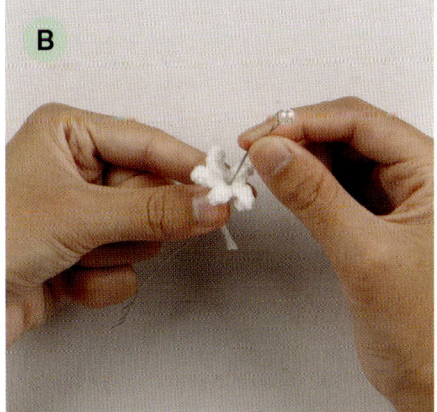

Tip

If pearls are unavailable, make the flower center by tying two knots with yellow yarn in the middle of the wire. Bend the wire in half and insert it into the flower.

Assembly

1. To make the flower center, insert a 20cm (8in) length of wire through the hole in a pearl bead (A), fold the wire, and thread it through the center of the flower (B). Wrap the wire with green yarn down to the end, securing it with glue (C). Using the same method, assemble all six flowers.

2. Fix the six flower branches to the top of the stem at varying heights (D), wrapping green yarn as you go. Wrap to the bottom of the stem and secure with glue (E).

Sweet Pea

YARN

Cotton or cotton blend, 4-ply in pink (5g / ¼oz), light pink (5g / ¼oz), green (10g / ½oz)

HOOK

2mm (US 4)

MATERIALS

0.5mm floral wire for small leaves: 6 x 20cm (8in) lengths

0.5mm floral wire for tendrils: 3 x 20cm (8in) lengths

0.5mm floral wire for flower centers: 4 x 20cm (8in) lengths

2mm floral stem: 1 x 40cm (16in) length

Hot glue gun

PATTERN NOTE:

This pattern uses the amigurumi method of working in a spiral. Join each round with a slst into the top of the first sc. It will help to use a stitch marker in the first stitch of the round, so that you know when you have completed the round. Move the marker up as you work.

LARGE PETAL

(MAKE 3)

Using light pink, make a magic ring.

Rnd 1: 1 ch (does not count as a st throughout), 6 sc into ring, join. (6 sts)

Rnd 2: [5 ch, 4 dtr] all into the next st, [3 dtr, 5 ch, 1 slst] all into the next st, skip 1 st, [1 slst, 5 ch, 4 dtr all into the next st, [3 dtr, 5 ch, 1 slst] all into the next st, skip 1 st, join with 1 slst into first st.

Fasten off and weave in the end.

SMALL PETAL

(MAKE 4)

Using pink, make a magic ring.

Rnd 1: [4 ch, 5 tr, 4 ch, 1 slst, 4 ch, 5 tr, 4 ch, 1 slst] all into ring. Tighten ring.

Fasten off and weave in the end.

FLOWER CENTER

(MAKE 4)

Using pink, ch 5.

Row 1: Starting in the 2nd ch from hook, 4 sc.

Fasten off.

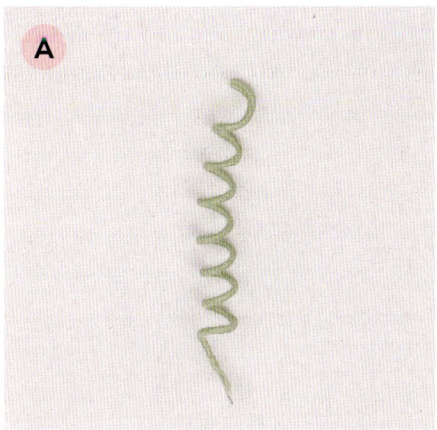
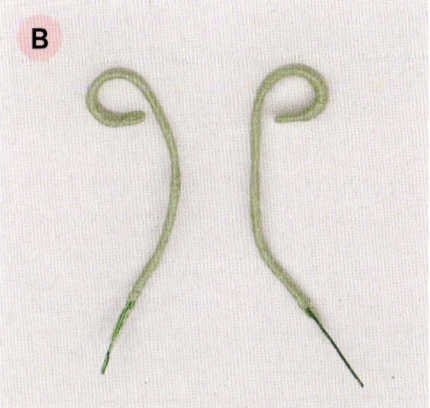

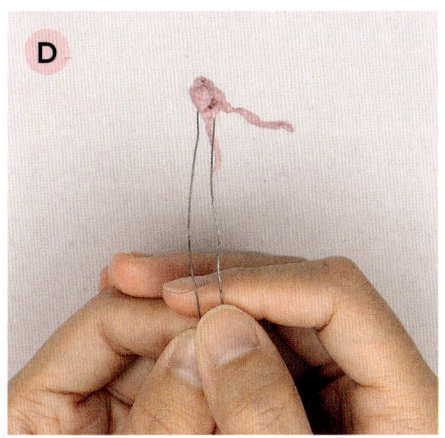
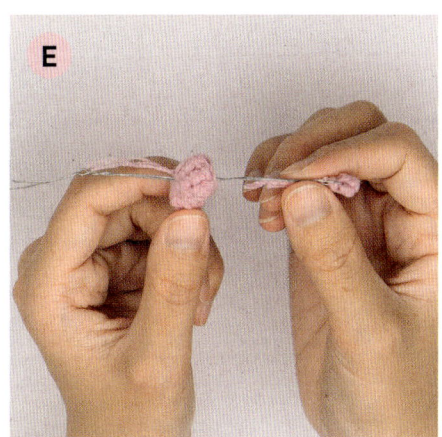
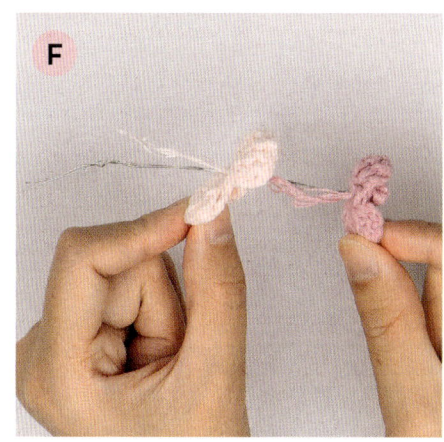

SMALL LEAF
(MAKE 6)

Using green, ch 8.

Rnd 1: Starting in the 2nd ch from hook, working over floral wire, 1 sc, 1 hdc, 3 dc, 1 hdc, [1 sc, ch 2- picot, 1 sc], rotate to work into opposite side of ch, 1 hdc, 3 dc, 1 hdc, 1 sc, join. (14 sts)

Fasten off and weave in the end.

ROUND LEAF
(MAKE 1)

Using green, make a magic ring.

Row 1: Working into ring, 4 ch, 16 tr, 4 ch, 1 slst. Tighten ring.

Fasten off.

Assembly

1. To make the tendrils, take three pieces of 20cm (8in) long floral wire and wrap green yarn around each of them separately, securing the end of the yarn. Then wrap one of the yarn-covered wires around your finger or a pencil a few times to create a spring-like shape (A). For the other two pieces, bend the top of the wire to create a round shape (B).

2. Use green yarn to wrap and secure two tendrils at the top of the floral stem. Continue wrapping for 4cm (1½in) before adding another tendril to the stem and wrapping the yarn to secure it.

3. Continue wrapping for 2cm (¾in), then add small leaves to both sides of the floral stem (C).

4. Fold the flower center in half and thread a 20cm (8in) piece of floral wire through it (D). Then fold the wire in half and insert it into the center of a small petal to complete the small flower (F) Insert a small flower into the large petal (F) and wrap the wire with green yarn to assemble a large flower.

Tip

The method for making the tendrils is the same as that for the Morning Glory. Stretch or compress the coil to make it look as natural as possible.

5. Continue wrapping the stem with green yarn. Secure the small flower to the stem 2cm (¾in) below the leaves and wrap with yarn to fix it in place (G).

6. Group the three large flowers together (H) and attach them to the other side of the floral stem, securing with yarn (I).

7. Add a round leaf at a 1cm interval, wrap down to the end of the floral stem, and glue to secure (J).

Morning Glory

YARN

Cotton or cotton blend, 4-ply in white (10g / ½oz), green (15g / ¾oz), blue (5g / ¼oz), yellow (2g / ¼oz)

HOOK

2mm (US 4)

MATERIALS

0.5mm floral wire for leaves: 4 x 20cm (8in) lengths

0.5mm floral wire for tendril : 4 x 20cm (8in) lengths

0.5mm floral wire for flower centers : 4 x 20cm (8in) lengths

0.5mm floral wire for bud: 1 x 15cm (6in) length

3mm floral stem: 1 x 40cm (16in) length

Fiberfill stuffing

Hot glue gun

PATTERN NOTE:

This pattern uses the amigurumi method of working in a spiral. Join each round with a slst into the top of the first sc. It will help to use a stitch marker in the first stitch of the round, so that you know when you have completed the round. Move the marker up as you work.

COLOR CHANGE:

Change to next color on the last yo of the previous stitch.

FLOWER
(MAKE 2)

Using green, make a magic ring.

Rnd 1: 1 ch (does not count as a st throughout), 6 sc into ring, join. (6 sts)

Rnds 2–3: 1 ch, 6 sc, join.

Rnd 4: 1 ch, [2 sc, 2 sc in the next st] twice, join. (8 sts)

Rnd 5: Working in FLO, 2 ch, 1 dc2tog, 3-ch picot, 2 ch, * 1 slst, 2 ch, 1 dc2tog (placing first st of dc2tog in same st as previous slst), 3-ch picot, 2 ch; repeat from * 3 more times, 1 slst.

Change to white.

Rnd 6: Working in BLO of Rnd 4, 8 sc, join. (8 sts)

Rnd 7: 1 ch, 8 sc, join.

Rnd 8: 1 ch, [3 sc, 2 sc in the next st] twice, join. (10 sts)

Rnd 9: 1 ch, 10 sc, join.

Rnd 10: 1 ch, [4 sc, 2 sc in the next st] twice, join. (12 sts)

Rnd 11: 1 ch, 12 sc, join.

Rnd 12: 1 ch, [3 sc, 2 sc in the next st] 3 times, join. (15 sts)

Rnd 13: 1 ch, [change to blue, 2 sc, change to white, 2 sc in the next st] 5 times, join. (20 sts)

Rnd 14: 1 ch, [change to blue, 3 sc, change to white, 2 sc in the next st] 5 times, join. (25 sts)

Rnd 15: 1 ch, [change to blue, 4 sc, change to white, 2 sc in the next st] 5 times, join. (30 sts)

Rnd 16: 1 ch, [change to blue, 5 sc, change to white, 2 sc in the next st] 5 times, join. (35 sts)

Rnd 17: 1 ch, * change to blue, 1 hdc, 2 dc in the next st, [1 dc, 1 hdc] in the next st, 1 sc, [1 hdc, 1 dc] in the next st, 2 dc in the next st, change to white, 1 sc; repeat from * 4 more times. (55 sts)

Fasten off and weave in the end.

BUD
(MAKE 1)

Using green, make a magic ring.

Rnds 1–5: Work as for flower.

Rnd 6: Change to white, 1 ch, working in BLO of Rnd 4, 8 sc, join. (8 sts)

Rnd 7: 1 ch, 8 sc, join.

Rnd 8: 1 ch, [3 sc, 2 sc in the next st] twice, join. (10 sts)

Rnd 9: 1 ch, 10 sc, join.

Change to blue.

Rnd 10: 1 ch, [4 sc, 2 sc in the next st] twice, join. (12 sts)

Rnd 11: 1 ch, 12 sc, join. (12 sts)

Rnd 12: 1 ch, [3 sc, 1 sc2tog] twice, 2 sc, join. (10 sts)

Rnds 13–15: 1 ch, 10 sc, join.

Rnd 16: 1 ch, 1 sc, 1 sc2tog, 2 sc, 1 sc2tog, 1 sc, 1 sc2tog, join. (7 sts)

Rnd 17: 1 ch, 7 sc.

Add some fiberfill.

Rnd 18: 1 ch, 3 sc2tog, 1 sc, join. (4 sts)

Fasten off.

LEAF
(MAKE 4)

Using green, ch 15.

Rnd 1: Starting in the 2nd ch from hook, working over floral wire, 1 sc, 1 hdc, 9 dc, 1 hdc, 1 sc, 3 sc in the next st, rotate to work into the opposite side of ch, 1 sc, 1 hdc, 9 dc, 1 hdc, 1 sc, join. (29 sts)

Rnd 2: 1 ch, 3 sc, 3 hdc, 2 dc in the next st, [1 tr, 2ch-picot, 3 ch, 1 slst] all into the next st, 6 slst, [1 slst, 2 ch] in the next st, 6 slst, [5 ch , starting in the 3rd ch from hook, 1 slst, 1 tr], 2 dc in the next st, 3 hdc, 3 sc, join.

Fasten off and weave in the end.

Assembly

1. To make the tendril, take a 20cm (8in) length of floral wire and wrap green yarn around it, twisting the end of the wire to secure the yarn. Then wrap the yarn-covered wire around your finger or a pencil a few times to create a spring-like shape (A).

2. Thread a 15cm (6in) length of floral wire through the base of the bud, fold in half, wrap with green yarn, and twist the wire to secure the yarn.

3. Wrap and secure the bud and tendril with green yarn at the top of the floral stem (B).

4. To make a stamen, divide a 30cm (12in) piece of yellow 4-ply into two strands of 2-ply. Wrap 2-ply around a 20cm (8in) piece of floral wire. Fold in half to form the stamen shape (C) and twist the wire to secure the base. Repeat to make five stamens.

5. Bind two stamens together to form a large stamen (D). Insert into flower, wrap with green yarn, and twist the wire to secure the yarn (E).

6. Continue wrapping the stem with green yarn. Add a leaf to the stem 3cm (1¼in) below the twig and secure with yarn. At 1cm (½in) interval, add a flower on the other side of the stem (F).

7. Continue adding the remaining flowers and leaves in the positions shown (G).

8. Finish wrapping to the base and secure the end with glue (H).

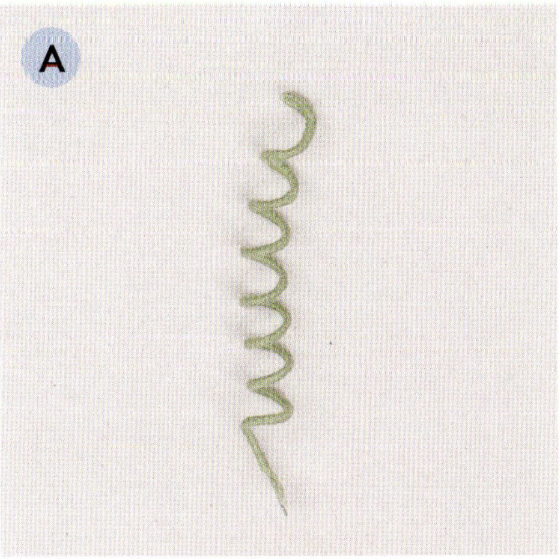

A	B	C
D	E
F	G	H

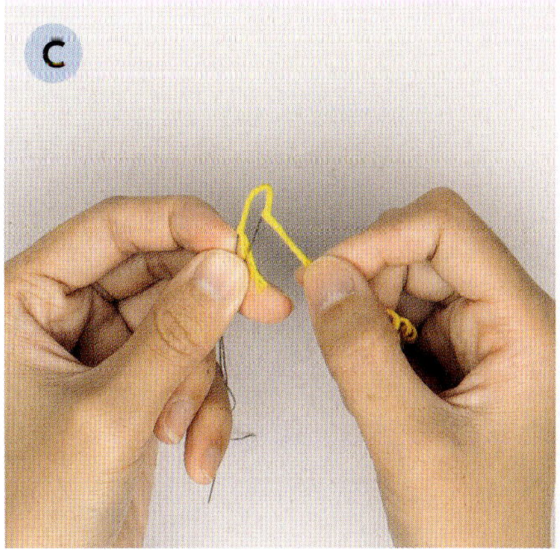

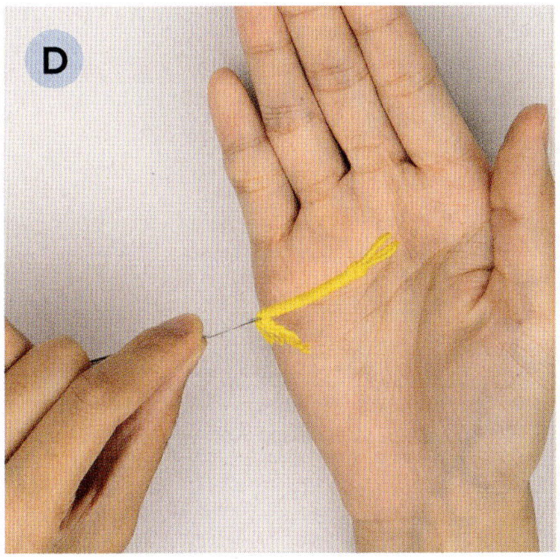

Tip

This versatile method for making a morning glory flower center is also used for Lily of the Valley and Lantern Lilies.

Bell Flower

YARN

Cotton or cotton blend, 4-ply in purple (10g / ½oz), white (5g / ¼oz), green (10g / ½oz), yellow (2g / ¼oz)

HOOK

2mm (US 4)

MATERIALS

0.5mm floral wire for flower centers: 5 x 10cm (4in) lengths

2mm floral stem: 1 x 40cm (16in) length

Hot glue gun

PATTERN NOTE:

This pattern uses the amigurumi method of working in a spiral. Join each round with a slst into the top of the first sc. It will help to use a stitch marker in the first stitch of the round, so that you know when you have completed the round. Move the marker up as you work.

GRADIENT FLOWER

(MAKE 2)

Using white, make a magic ring.

Rnd 1: 1 ch (does not count as a st throughout), 5 sc into ring, join. (5 sts)

Rnd 2: 1 ch, [2 sc in the next st] 5 times, join. (10 sts)

Rnd 3: 1 ch, [1 sc, 2 sc in the next st] 5 times, join. (15 sts)

Rnd 4: 1 ch, 15 sc, join.

Rnds 5–8: 1 ch, [1 FPsc, 2 sc] 5 times, join.

Rnd 9: Change to purple, * 1 FPsc, skip 1 st, [1 hdc, 1 dc, 1 ch, 1 dc, 1 hdc] all into the next st; repeat from * 4 more times. (5 petals)

Fasten off and weave in the end.

PURPLE FLOWER

(MAKE 3)

With purple, make as for gradient flower.

CALYX

(MAKE 6)

Using green, make a magic ring.

Rnd 1: 1 ch, 5 sc into ring, join. (5 sts)

Rnd 2: 1 ch, [2 sc in the next st] 5 times, join. (10 sts)

Rnd 3: 1 ch, [1 sc, 2 sc in the next st] 5 times, join. (15 sts)

Rnd 4: * 7 ch, starting in the 2nd ch from hook, 1 slst, 2 sc, 3 hdc, skip 2 st, 1 slst; repeat from * 4 more times.

Fasten off and weave in the end.

Assembly

1. To make a flower center, split 4-ply yellow yarn into 2-ply and wrap 2-ply yarn around a 10cm (4in) length of wire (A). Fold it in half to form the stamen shape (B), finish wrapping with white yarn (C), and secure it by twisting the end of the wire. Repeat to make five flower centers.

2. Insert the flower center into the flower (D), slip the calyx over the wire and glue it to the flower, then wrap the wire in yarn (E).

3. Attach the five flowers sequentially to the stem, securing each with yarn (F). Finally, apply glue to secure the end.

Calla Lily

YARN

Cotton or cotton blend, 4-ply in white (10g / ½oz), green (10g / ½oz), yellow (2g / ¼oz)

HOOK

2mm (US 4)

MATERIALS

0.5mm floral wire for leaf: 1 x 30cm (12in) length

3mm floral stem: 1 x 40cm (16in) length

Hot glue gun

PATTERN NOTE:

This pattern uses the amigurumi method of working in a spiral. Join each round with a slst into the top of the first sc. It will help to use a stitch marker in the first stitch of the round, so that you know when you have completed the round. Move the marker up as you work.

FLOWER

(MAKE 1)

Using white, make a magic ring.

Rnd 1: 1 ch (does not count as a st throughout), 10 sc into ring, join. (10 sts)

Rnd 2: 3 ch (does not count as a st throughout), [2 dc in the next st] 10 times, join. (20 sts)

Rnd 3: 1 ch, [3 sc, 2 sc in the next st] twice, [1 sc, 2 sc in the next st] twice, [3 sc, 2 sc in the next st] twice, join. (26 sts)

Rnd 4: 1 ch, [4 sc, 2 sc in the next st] twice, [2 sc, 2 sc in the next st] twice, [4 sc, 2 sc in the next st] twice, join. (32 sts)

Rnd 5: 1 ch, 5 sc, 2 sc in the next st, [2 sc, 2 sc in the next st] twice, [3 sc, 2 sc in the next st] twice, [2 sc, 2 sc in the next st] twice, 5 sc, 2 sc in the next st, join. (40 sts)

Rnd 6: 2 ch, 6 hdc, 2 hdc in the next st, [3 hdc, 2 hdc in the next st] twice, [4 hdc, 2 hdc in the next st] twice, [3 hdc, 2 hdc in the next st] twice, 7 hdc, join. (47)

Rnd 7: 3 ch, 7 dc, [2 dc in the next st] 16 times, [1 tr, 4 ch, starting in the 2nd ch from hook, 3 slst, 1 tr] all into the next st, [2 dc in the next st] 16 times, 5 dc, place st marker in last st made, 2 dc, join. (80 sts)

Join green in marked st on Rnd 7.

Now work in rows.

Row 1: 2 ch, 5 hdc, leave remaining sts unworked, turn. (5 sts)

Row 2: 2 ch, 5 hdc.

Fasten off and weave in the end.

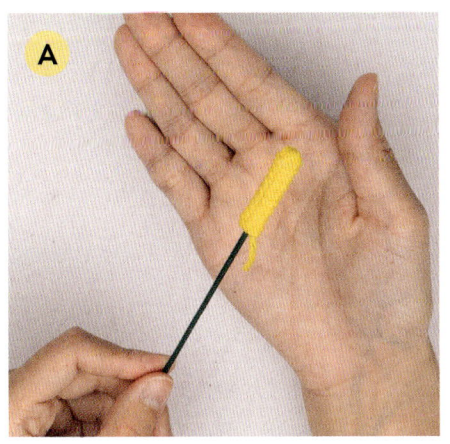 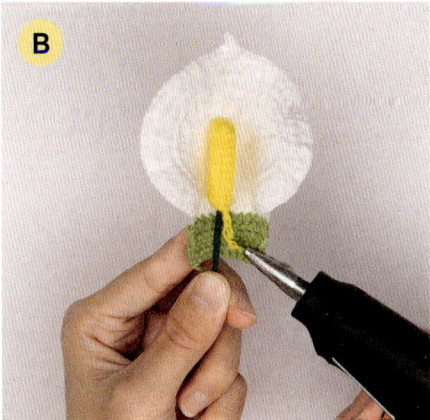 

FLOWER CENTER
(MAKE 1)

Using yellow, make a magic ring.

Rnds 1–10: 1 ch, 6 sc, join. (6 sts)

Fasten off and weave in the end.

LEAF
(MAKE 1)

Using green, ch 31.

Rnd 1: Starting in the 2nd ch from hook, 3 sc, 3 hdc, 18 dc, 3 hdc, 2 sc, 3 sc in the next st, rotate to work into opposite side of ch, 2 sc, 3 hdc, 18 dc, 3 hdc, 3 sc, join. (61 sts)

Rnd 2: Working over a 30cm (12in) piece of floral wire, sc in every st around, join.

Fasten off and weave in the end.

Assembly

1. Apply glue to the top of the floral stem and insert the flower center into it (A).

2. Place the flower center in the flower. Apply glue to the green part of the flower and wrap it around the center (B).

3. Wrap green yarn around the base of the calyx for about 5cm (2in). Add leaves and secure them with yarn (C). Finally, apply glue to the end of the floral stem to fix the yarn in place.

FOLIAGE

Foliage plays a crucial role in floral arrangements, enhancing the design's aesthetic and structure. It creates a backdrop that highlights and complements the flowers. As a supportive framework that holds the arrangement together, foliage stabilizes the flowers and ensures the bouquet or centerpiece maintains its shape.

Fern Leaf

YARN
Cotton or cotton blend, 4-ply in green (15g / ¾oz)

HOOK
2mm (US 4)

MATERIALS
0.5mm floral wire for leaf: 3x15cm, 2 x10 cm, 4x8 cm lengths

2mm floral stem: 1 x 40cm (16in) length

Hot glue gun

PATTERN NOTE:
You will work all sc over the floral wire for the first side of each leaf, then fold the wire and work over the wire and into the underside of the sts of the first side to complete the second side. Leave 5cm (2in) of wire sticking out at the start.

PART A
(MAKE 1)

Using green, ch 26.

Row 1: Starting in the 2nd ch from hook, working over floral wire, 1 sc, 10 ch, starting in the 2nd ch from hook, 9 slst, 1 sc.

Row 2: 1 sc, 9 ch, starting in the 2nd ch from hook, 8 slst, 1 sc.

Row 3: 1 sc, 8 ch, starting in the 2nd ch from hook, 7 slst, 1 sc.

Rows 4–5: 1 sc, 7 ch, starting in the 2nd ch from hook, 6 slst, 1 sc.

Row 6: 1 sc, 6 ch, starting in the 2nd ch from hook, 5 slst, 1 sc.

Row 7: 1 sc, 5 ch, starting in the 2nd ch from hook, 4 slst, 1 sc.

Rows 8–10: 1 sc, 4 ch, starting in the 2nd ch from hook, 3 slst, 1 sc.

Rows 11–12: 1 sc, 3 ch, starting in the 2nd ch from hook, 2 slst, 1 sc.

Row 13: (Leaf apex) 1 sc, 3 ch, starting in the 2nd ch from hook, 2 slst, 1 sc in next ch (this is the first sc of other side the leaf).

To work the other side of the leaf, fold the floral wire in half, then repeat Rows 11 down to Row 1, working over the floral wire and into the underside of the sts of Rows 1 to 11. The patterns for both sides are symmetrical.

Fasten off and weave in the end.

PART B
(MAKE 2)

Using green, ch 8.

Row 1: Starting in the 2nd ch from hook, working over floral wire, 1 sc, 4 ch, starting in the 2nd ch from hook, 3 slst, 1 sc.

Rows 2–3: 1 sc, 4 ch, starting in the 2nd ch from hook, 3 slst, 1 sc.

Row 4: (Leaf apex) 1 sc, 4 ch, starting in the 2nd ch from hook, 3 slst, 1 sc in next ch (this is the first sc of other side the leaf).

Rows 5–7: To work the other side of the leaf, fold the floral wire in half, then repeat Rows 1 to 3 working over the floral wire and into the underside of the sts of Rows 1 to 3.

Fasten off and weave in the end.

PART C
(MAKE 2)

Using green, ch 10.

Row 1: Starting in the 2nd ch from hook, working over floral wire, 1 sc, 5 ch, starting in the 2nd ch from hook, 4 slst, 1 sc.

Row 2: 1 sc, 5 ch, starting in the 2nd ch from hook, 4 slst, 1 sc.

Rows 3–4: 1 sc, 4 ch, starting in the 2nd ch from hook, 3 slst, 1 sc.

Row 5: (Leaf apex) 1 sc, 4 ch, starting in the 2nd ch from hook, 3 slst, 1 sc in next ch (this is the first sc of other side the leaf).

To work the other side of the leaf, fold the floral wire in half, then work over the floral wire and into the underside of the sts of Rows 1 to 4:

Rows 6–7: 1 sc, 4 ch, starting in the 2nd ch from hook, 3 slst, sc.

Rows 8–9: 1 sc, 5 ch, starting in the 2nd ch from hook, 4 slst, sc.

Fasten off and weave in the end.

PART D
(MAKE 2)

Using green, ch 16.

Row 1: Starting in the 2nd ch from hook, working over floral wire, 1 sc, 6 ch, starting in the 2nd ch from hook, 5 slst, 1 sc.

Rows 2–3: 1 sc, 6 ch, starting in the 2nd ch from hook, 5 slst, 1 sc.

Rows 4–5: 1 sc, 5 ch, starting in the 2nd ch from hook, 4 slst, 1 sc

Rows 6–7: 1 sc, 4 ch, starting in the 2nd ch from hook, 3 slst, 1 sc.

Row 8: (Leaf apex) 1 sc, 4 ch, starting in the 2nd ch from hook, 3 slst, 1 sc in next ch (this is the first sc of other side the leaf).

To work the other side of the leaf, fold the floral wire in half, then repeat Row 7 down to Row 1, working over the floral wire and into the underside of the sts of Rows 1 to 7. The patterns for both sides are symmetrical.

Fasten off and weave in the end.

PART E
(MAKE 2)

Using green, ch 20.

Row 1: Starting in the 2nd ch from hook, working over floral wire, 1 sc, 7 ch, starting in the 2nd ch from hook, 6 slst, 1 sc.

Row 2: 1 sc, 8 ch, starting in the 2nd ch from hook, 7 slst, 1 sc.

Rows 3–4: 1 sc, 7 ch, starting in the 2nd ch from hook, 6 slst, 1 sc.

Row 5: 1 sc, 6 ch, starting in the 2nd ch from hook, 5 slst, 1 sc.

Rows 6–7: 1 sc, 5 ch, starting in the 2nd ch from hook, 4 slst, 1 sc.

Rows 8–9: 1 sc, 4 ch, starting in the 2nd ch from hook, 3 slst, 1 sc.

Row 10: (Leaf apex) 1 sc, 4 ch, starting in the 2nd ch from hook, 3 slst, 1 sc in next ch (this is the first sc of other side the leaf).

To work the other side of the leaf, repeat Row 9 down to Row 1, working over the floral wire and into the underside of the sts of Rows 1 to 9. The patterns for both sides are symmetrical.

Fasten off and weave in the end.

Assembly

1. Place part A at the top of the floral stem and secure it by wrapping green yarn around it, fixing it to the stem (A).

2. Continue wrapping the floral stem for about 1 cm (½in). Place parts B on either side of the stem, fixing them in place with wrapped yarn (B).

3. Using the same method, attach parts C, D, and E (C, D, E). Continue wrapping the wire down to the end of the stem and secure it with glue.

Ginkgo Leaf

YARN

Cotton or cotton blend, 4-ply in light brown (5g / ¼oz) and yellow (12g / ½oz)

HOOK

2mm (US 4)

MATERIALS

0.5mm floral wire for leaves: 12 x 20cm (8in) lengths

0.5mm floral wire for fruits: 3 x 20cm (8in) lengths

2mm floral stem: 1 x 40cm (16in) length

Hot glue gun

PATTERN NOTE:

The leaves start by working into a magic ring over floral wire. They are then worked in rows.

This pattern uses the amigurumi method of working in a spiral. Join each round with a slst into the top of the first sc. It will help to use a stitch marker in the first stitch of the round, so that you know when you have completed the round. Move the marker up as you work.

LARGE LEAF
(MAKE 5)

Using yellow, make a magic ring.

Row 1 (RS): 3 ch (does not count as a st throughout), working over floral wire, 10 dc into ring, tighten ring, turn. (10 sts)

Row 2: 1 ch (does not count as a st throughout), 10 sc, join.

Row 3: 4 ch, [2 tr in the next st] 4 times, [1 tr, 2 ch, 1 sc] all into the next st, [1 sc, 2 ch, 1 tr] all into the next st, [2 tr in the next st] 3 times, [2 tr in the next st, 4 ch, 1 slst] all into the next st. (20 sts)

Fasten off and weave in the end.

MEDIUM LEAF
(MAKE 5)

Using yellow, make a magic ring.

Row 1 (RS): Working over floral wire, 3 ch, 10 dc into ring, tighten ring, turn. (10 sts)

Row 2: 2 ch, [2 dc in the next st] 4 times, [1 dc, 1 ch, 1 slst] all into the next st, [1 slst, 1 ch, 1 dc] all into the next st, [2 dc in the next st] 3 times, [2 dc in the next st, 2 ch, 1 slst] all into the next st . (20 sts)

Fasten off and weave in the end.

SMALL LEAF
(MAKE 2)

Using yellow, make a magic ring.

Row 1 (RS): Working over floral wire, 3 ch, 10 dc into ring, tighten ring, turn. (10 sts)

Row 2: 1 ch, [2 dc in the next st] 4 times, [1 sc, 1ch, 1 slst] all into the next st, [1 slst, 1 ch, 1 sc] all into the next st, [2 dc in the next st] 3 times, [2 dc in the next st, 1 ch, 1 slst] all into the next st. (20 sts)

Fasten off and weave in the end.

GINKGO FRUIT
(MAKE 3)

Using yellow, make a magic ring.

Rnd 1: 1 ch, 5 sc into ring, join. (5 sts)

Rnd 2: 1 ch [2 sc in next st] 5 times, join. (10 sts)

Rnd 3: 1 ch, [1 sc, 2 sc in next st] 5 times, join. (15 sts)

Rnds 4–6: 1 ch, 15 sc, join. (15 sts)

Rnd 7: 1 ch, [1 sc, 1 sc2tog] 5 times, join. (10 sts)

Rnd 8: 1 ch, 5 sc2tog. (5 sts)

Fasten off and leave a long tail to wrap the wire.

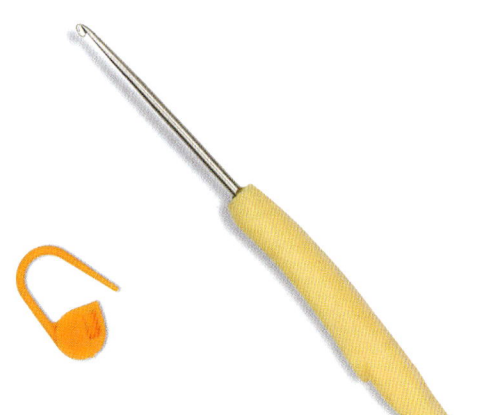

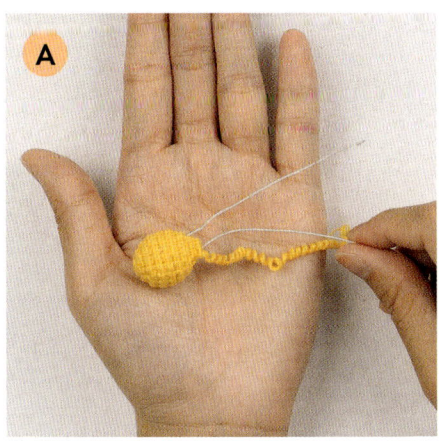

Assembly

1. Insert a 20cm (8in) wire into the base of the ginkgo fruit and fold it in half. Wrap the wire with the yarn tail and twist the end of the wire to secure the yarn (A).

2. To assemble branch one, combine two medium leaves, one large leaf, and one ginkgo fruit, and secure them together with light brown yarn (B).

3. Assemble branch two by combining two large leaves, one medium leaf, one small leaf, and one ginkgo fruit, and secure them together with light brown yarn (C).

4. Combine one large leaf, one medium leaf, one small leaf, and one ginkgo fruit, and secure them with light brown yarn at the top of the floral stem (D).

5. Continue wrapping the stem in light brown yarn, adding one large leaf and one medium leaf at 5cm (2in) intervals then securing them with yarn (E).

6. Wrap the yarn for about 5cm (2in), then add branch one and branch two, securing them with yarn. Wrap the yarn down to the base of the stem and glue the end to secure it (F).

Common Leaf

YARN
Cotton or cotton blend, 4-ply in green (10g / ½oz)

HOOK
2mm (US 4)

MATERIALS
0.6mm floral wire for leaves: 7 x 30cm (12in) length

0.5mm floral stem: 1 x 40cm (16in) length

Hot glue gun

PATTERN NOTE:
After each Round, slst into the first sc and ch 1. This ch 1 does not count as a st – continue the next Round on the next stitches.

LEAF
(MAKE 7)

Using green, ch 12.

Rnd 1: Starting in the 2nd ch from hook, working over floral wire, 1 sc, 1 hdc, 2 dc, 3 tr, 2 dc, 1 hdc, 3 sc in the next st, rotate to work into opposite side of ch, 1 hdc, 2 dc, 3 tr, 2 dc, 1 hdc, 1 sc, join. (23 sts)

Fasten off and weave in the end.

Tip
You can freely adjust the number of leaves you add and change their arrangement to create the different types of foliage a bouquet might need.

Assembly

1. Attach the first leaf to the top of the stem and secure it with yarn (A).

2. At 5cm (2in) intervals down the stem, place two leaves on each side, wrapping yarn to secure them (B, C).

3. Continue wrapping the yarn to the bottom of the stem, then secure the end with glue (D).

Orchid Leaf

YARN
Cotton or cotton blend, 4-ply in green (15g / ¾oz)

HOOK
2mm (US 4)

MATERIALS
0.6mm floral wire for leaves: 4 x 30cm (12in) length

0.5mm floral stem: 1 x 40cm (16in) length

Hot glue gun

LEAF
(MAKE 4)

Using green, ch 60.

Rnd 1: Starting in the 2nd ch from hook, working over floral wire, 3 sc, 52 hdc, 3 sc, 3 sc in the next st, rotate to work into opposite side of ch, 3 sc, 52 hdc, 3 sc, join. (119 sts)

Fasten off and weave in the end.

Assembly

1. Attach two leaves to the top of the stem and secure them with green yarn (A).

2. Continue wrapping down the stem with yarn, adding one leaf every 1cm (½in) and securing it with yarn. When you reach the bottom of the stem, apply glue to fix the end (B, C).

Tip

Slender leaves add a sense of structure and movement to a bouquet, making it more dynamic. They are a versatile choice for layering with statement flowers.

Northern Sea Oats

YARN
Cotton or cotton blend, 4-ply in green (8g / ½oz)

HOOK
1.5mm (US 8/7/2)

MATERIALS
0.5mm floral wire for leaves: 13 x 20cm (8in) lengths

2mm floral stem: 1 x 40cm (16in) length

Hot glue gun

PATTERN NOTE:
The stitch used here to make the leaves is called Tunisian Simple Stitch.

LEAF
(MAKE 13)

Using green, ch 8.

Row 1 (RS) (forward pass): Starting in the 2nd ch from hook, [insert hook into ch, pull up loop in ch] 7 times. (8 loops on hook) (A)

Row 1 (return pass): [Yo, pull through 2 loops] until 1 loop remains (B)

Turn piece over to work into opposite side of ch.

Row 2 (WS) (forward pass): Working into unused loops of ch, [insert hook into ch, pull up loop in ch] 7 times. (8 loops on hook) (C)

Row 2 (return pass): [Yo, pull through 2 loops] until 1 loop remains.

Turn piece over so that RS is facing, insert hook into first loop, yo and draw through both loops on hook (D). After the last stitch, pull out the loop, cut the yarn and secure the leaf tip with a small dot of glue.

Assembly

1. Take a 0.5mm, 20cm (8in) wire and place one leaf at its top (E). Wrap the yarn around the wire to secure the leaf. Continue adding a leaf every 6cm (2½in) (F), assembling a total of three leaves on this branch. Repeat this process to create three branches, each with three leaves. Then make two branches with two leaves each, following the same method (G).

2. Assemble the six branches at varying heights on a 2mm floral stem. Wrap green yarn around the stem to secure the branches (H). When you reach the bottom, apply glue to fix the yarn securely (I).

Mint Leaf

YARN

Cotton or cotton blend, 4-ply in green (8g / ½oz)

HOOK

1.5mm (US 8/7/2)

MATERIALS

0.6mm floral wire for large leaves: 4 x 12cm (4¾in) lengths

0.6mm floral wire for medium leaves: 2 x 10cm (4in) lengths

2mm floral stem: 1 x 40cm (16in) length

Hot glue gun

PATTERN NOTE:

After each Round, slst into the first sc and ch 1. This ch 1 does not count as a st – continue the next Round on the next stitches.

LARGE LEAF

(MAKE 14)

Using green, ch 16.

Rnd 1: Starting in the 2nd ch from hook, working over a 12cm (4¾in) piece of floral wire, 1 sc, 1 hdc, 1 dc, [1 tr2tog, 1ch-picot] 4 times, 1 dc, 1 hdc, 1 sc, 3 sc in the next st, rotate to work into opposite side of ch, 1 sc, 1 hdc, 1 dc, [1 tr2tog, 1ch-picot] 4 times, 1 dc, 1 hdc, 1 sc, join. (31 sts)

Fasten off and weave in the end.

MEDIUM LEAF

(MAKE 2)

Using green, ch 4.

Rnd 1: Starting in the 2nd ch from hook, working over a 10cm (4in) piece of floral wire, 1 hdc, 1ch-picot, [1 dc, 1ch-picot] 3 times all into the next st, [1 dc, 1ch-picot] 6 times all into the next st, rotate to work into opposite side of ch, [1 dc, 1ch-picot] 3 times all into the next st, 1 hdc, join. (27 sts)

Fasten off and weave in the end.

SMALL LEAF

(MAKE 2)

Using green.

Rnd 1: * 6 ch, starting in the 2nd ch from hook, 1 slst, 1 hdc, 1 dc, 1 hdc, 1 slst; repeat from * once more, join.

Fasten off and weave in the end.

Assembly

1. Apply glue to the top of the floral stem, place the small leaf on it, and secure it by wrapping with green yarn (A).

2. Secure the two medium leaves directly below the small leaf, ensuring they are closely attached to the base of the small leaf (B).

3. Continue by adding four large leaves, wrapping the wire around the stem to secure them in place (C).

4. Wrap green yarn around the stem down to the bottom, then secure the end with glue (D).

Cordyline Fruticosa

YARN

Cotton or cotton blend, 4-ply in green (12g / ½oz) and cream (5g / ¼oz)

HOOK

2mm (US 4)

MATERIALS

0.6mm floral wire for leaf: 1 x 40cm (16in) length

2mm floral stem: 1 x 40cm (16in) length

Hot glue gun

PATTERN NOTE:

This pattern uses the amigurumi method of working in a spiral. Join each round with a slst into the top of the first sc. It will help to use a stitch marker in the first stitch of the round, so that you know when you have completed the round. Move the marker up as you work.

SPECIAL STITCHES:

Spike stitch: Instead of inserting the hook into the top of the next stitch on the current row, insert it into a stitch or space in a lower row. For example, if you're on Row 3, you might insert your hook into a stitch in Row 2 or 1.

Yarn over and pull up a loop, drawing it up to the height of the current row. This forms the 'spike'. Finish the stitch by yarning over and pulling through the loops on your hook as you would in a regular stitch, such as single crochet or double crochet.

LEAF

(MAKE 1)

Using green, ch 50. (A)

Rnd 1: Starting in the 2nd ch from hook, 3 sc, 3 hdc, 3 dc, 30 tr, 3 dc, 3 hdc, 3 sc, 3 sc in the next st, rotate to work into opposite side of ch, 3 sc, 3 hdc, 3 dc, 30 tr, 3 dc, 3 hdc, 3 sc, join. (99 sts) (A, B)

Rnd 2: Working over floral wire, 6 sc, 6 hdc, 3 dc, 20 tr, 3 dc, 6 hdc, 5 sc, 3 sc in the next st, 5 sc, 6 hdc, 3 dc, 20 tr, 3 dc, 6 hdc, 6 sc, join. (101 sts) (C)

Rnd 3: Change to cream, 1 sc in every st around. You can work a spike stitch every 3 to 6 sts to create a patterned effect. (D, E, F)

Tip
After the last st, slst to join. Before cutting the yarn, enlarge the loop, pass it over the wire and tighten it. This will securely wrap the wire and yarn (E).

Assembly

1. Place the leaf at the top of the floral stem and wrap green yarn around to make a secure join (G). Continue wrapping the yarn down to the base of the stem, then apply glue to secure the end (H).

Long Eucalyptus

YARN
Cotton or cotton blend, 4-ply in green (10g / ½oz)

HOOK
2mm (US 4)

MATERIALS
0.5mm floral wire for leaves: 1 x 50cm (19¾in) length

2mm floral stem: 1 x 25cm (10in) length

Hot glue gun

PATTERN NOTE:
This pattern uses the amigurumi method of working in a spiral. Join each round with a slst into the top of the first sc. It will help to use a stitch marker in the first stitch of the round, so that you know when you have completed the round. Move the marker up as you work.

LEAF A
(MAKE 2)

Using green, make a magic ring.

Rnd 1: Working into ring, 1 ch (does not count as a st throughout), 3 sc, 2 ch, 3 sc, tighten ring, join.

Fasten off and weave in the end.

LEAF B
(MAKE 2)

Using green, make a magic ring.

Rnd 1: 1 ch, 6 sc into ring, join. (6 sts)

Rnd 2: 1 ch, [2 sc in the next st] 6 times, join. (12 sts)

Fasten off and weave in the end.

LEAF C
(MAKE 3)

Using green, make a magic ring.

Rnd 1: 1 ch, 7 sc into ring, join. (7 sts)

Rnd 2: 1 ch, [2 sc in the next st] 7 times, join. (14 sts)

Fasten off and weave in the end.

LEAF D
(MAKE 2)

Using green, make a magic ring.

Rnd 1: 1 ch, 7 sc into ring, join. (7 sts)

Rnd 2: 1 ch, [1 sc, 1 hdc] all into the next st, [2 hdc in the next st] twice, [1 hdc, 1 dc, 1 hdc] all into the next st, [2 hdc in the next st] twice, [1 hdc, 1 sc] all into the next st, join. (15 sts)

Fasten off and weave in the end.

LEAF E
(MAKE 2)

Using green, make a magic ring.

Rnd 1: 1 ch, 8 sc into ring, join. (8 sts)

Rnd 2: 1 ch, [1 sc, 1 hdc] all into the next st, [3 dc in the next st] 3 times, 2 ch, [3 dc in the next st] 3 times, [1 hdc, 1 sc] all into the next st, join. (22 sts)

Fasten off and weave in the end.

Assembly

1. Take a 50cm (19¾in) piece of 0.5mm wire and fold it in half. Attach two leaf A pieces at the top of the wire and wrap them with green thread to secure (A). After a 3cm (1¼in) gap, add one leaf B, then after another 2cm (¾in), add another leaf B (B).

2. Continue wrapping the wire, adding one leaf C every 2cm (1in) (C).

3. Continue wrapping the wire, adding one leaf D every 2cm (¾in) (D).

4. Continue wrapping the wire, adding one leaf E every 2.5cm (1in) (E).

5. Attach the wire to the 25cm (10in) floral stem, wrapping it tightly with green yarn. Continue wrapping until you reach the bottom of the stem, then apply glue to fix the end securely (F).

Broad Eucalyptus

YARN

Cotton or cotton blend, 4-ply in green (10g / ½oz)

HOOK

1.5mm (US 8/7/2)

MATERIALS

0.6mm floral wire for leaves: 16 x 10cm (4in) lengths

0.5mm floral wire for branches: 6 x 20cm (8in) lengths

2mm floral stem: 1 x 20cm (8in) length

Hot glue gun

PATTERN NOTE:

After each Round, slst into the first sc and ch 1. This ch 1 does not count as a st – continue the next Round on the next stitches.

LEAF A

(MAKE 2)

Using green, ch 8.

Rnd 1: Starting in the 2nd ch from hook, working over floral wire, 1 sc, 1 hdc, 2 dc, [2 dc in the next st] twice, [1 tr, 1 hdc, 1 tr] in the next st, rotate to work into opposite side of ch, [2 dc in the next st] twice, 2 dc, 1 hdc, 1 sc, join. (19 sts)

Fasten off and weave in the end.

LEAF B

(MAKE 8)

Using green, ch 7.

Rnd 1: Starting in the 2nd ch from hook, working over floral wire, 1 sc, 1 hdc, 1 dc, [2 dc in the next st] twice, [1 dc, 1 sc, 1 dc] all into the next st, rotate to work into opposite side of ch, [2 dc in the next st] twice, 1 dc, 1 hdc, 1 sc, join. (17 sts)

Fasten off and weave in the end.

LEAF C

(MAKE 6)

Using green, ch 6.

Rnd 1: Starting in the 2nd ch from hook, working over floral wire, 1 sc, 1 hdc, 1 dc, 2 dc in the next st, [1 dc, 1 sc, 1 dc] all into the next st, 2 dc in the next st, 1 dc, 1 hdc, 1 sc, join. (13 sts)

Fasten off and weave in the end.

Assembly

1. Assemble the first branch by holding three 20cm (8in) pieces of 0.5mm wire together. Place two leaf B pieces at the top and secure with wire. Leave a 2cm (1in) gap, add another leaf B, and continue wrapping. Add another leaf B on the opposite side at an interval of approximately 1cm (½in). Then add a leaf C every 1.5cm (⅝in), for a total of three leaf C pieces (A).

2. Create a second branch with another three 20cm (8in) pieces of 0.5mm wire. Place two leaf A pieces at the top and secure them with green yarn (B). Then, at a 3cm (1¼in) interval, add a leaf B on the left side of the wire. Continue to add a leaf B every 1.5cm (⅝in), totaling three leaf B pieces (C). Then, add a leaf C every 1.5cm (⅝in), for a total of three leaf C pieces (D).

3. Take a 2mm, 20cm (8in) floral stem and attach the two branches to it (E). Wrap with green yarn to secure. At the bottom of the stem, apply glue to fix the yarn ends (F).

Maple Leaf

YARN
Cotton or cotton blend, 4-ply, in green (12g / ½oz)

HOOK
1.5mm (US 8/7/2)

MATERIALS
0.6mm floral wire for leaves: 21 x 10cm (4in) lengths

0.5mm floral wire for branches: 9 x 20cm (8in) lengths

2mm (US 4) floral stem: 1 x 20cm (8in) length

Hot glue gun

PATTERN NOTE:
After each Round, slst into the first sc and ch 1. This ch 1 does not count as a st – continue the next Round on the next stitches.

LARGE LEAF
(MAKE 9)

Using green, ch 15.

Rnd 1: Starting in the 2nd ch from hook, working over floral wire, 1 sc, 1 hdc, 1 dc, 5 tr, 2 dc, 2 hdc, 1 sc, [1 sc, 2ch-picot, 1 sc] all into the next ch, rotate to work into opposite side of ch, 1 sc, 2 hdc, 2 dc, 5 tr, 1 dc, 1 hdc, 1 sc, join. (29 sts)

Fasten off and weave in the end.

MEDIUM LEAF
(MAKE 6)

Using green, ch 13.

Rnd 1: Starting in the 2nd ch from hook, working over floral wire, 1 sc, 1 hdc, 6 dc, 2 hdc, 1 sc, [1 sc, 2ch-picot, 1 sc] in the next st, rotate to work into opposite side of ch, 1 sc, 2 hdc, 6 dc, 1 hdc, 1 sc, join. (25 sts)

Fasten off and weave in the end.

SMALL LEAF
(MAKE 6)

Using green, ch 9.

Rnd 1: Starting in the 2nd ch from hook, working over floral wire, 1 sc, 1 hdc, 2 dc, 2 hdc, 1 sc, [1 sc, 2ch-picot, 1 sc] in the next st, rotate to work into opposite side of ch, 1 sc, 2 hdc, 2 dc, 1 hdc, 1 sc, join. (17 sts)

Fasten off and weave in the end.

> **Tip**
> Use thicker wire for the main stem and thinner wire for the side branches. If a single wire for a side branch is too thin, fix 2 to 3 thin wires together for added strength.

Assembly

1. Hold three 20cm (8in) pieces of 0.5mm wire together. Secure three large leaves, two medium leaves, and two small leaves at the top of the wires, wrapping with green yarn to fix them in place. The order should be large leaves in the center, with medium and small leaves on each side (A). Repeat this process to assemble a total of three branches.

2. Take one of the branches and wrap the yarn around it for 12cm (4¾in) (B). On its right side, add another branch at a slightly lower height and wrap the yarn to secure it (C). Continue wrapping for another 3cm (1¼in), then add the third branch on the left side, positioning it at a lower height than the other two branches (D). Secure it by wrapping the yarn.

3. Take the three assembled branches and secure them together onto a 25cm (10in) floral stem. Wrap the yarn around the stem, fixing the branches in place until you reach the bottom of the stem (E). Apply glue to secure the end of the yarn.

BOUQUET IDEAS

Rarely does a week go by without some special occasion taking place — the birth of a baby, an anniversary, or a dinner party. Or perhaps a holiday, like Valentine's Day or Mother's Day. Whatever the event, flowers often play an essential role in the celebration.

It has been said that flowers speak an international language, understood by all peoples of the world. When designing a floral arrangement, consider the message you want the bouquet to 'speak' to the recipient. Understanding the meaning will help you successfully select the right flowers and foliage, as well as the container and accessories. Together, these will achieve the overall look and feel you want to convey with your bouquet.

WEDDING
Bouquet

A hand-tied bouquet is one of the most popular and versatile wedding styles. It is characterized by a loose, natural arrangement and stems that are bound together by ribbon, twine, or fabric. This type of bouquet has a relaxed, organic feel, making it perfect for outdoor ceremonies.

FLOWERS AND FOLIAGE USED IN THIS ARRANGEMENT:

FLOWERS

FOCAL FLOWERS

Hyacinth: 1 stem, orange and yellow

Classic Rose: 2 stems, orange and yellow

Epiphyllum: 1 stem, orange and yellow

SECONDARY FLOWERS

Tulip: 3 stems, orange

Plum Blossom: 1 stem, green and yellow

FILLER FLOWERS

Baby's Breath: 2 stems, red

Winter Berry: 2 stems, red

FOLIAGE

Fern Leaf: 1 stem, green yellow

MATERIALS

Adhesive tape

Beige ruffle ribbon: 1 x 40cm (16in) length

ASSEMBLY

1. First determine the position of the main flowers. Start by placing the Epiphyllum, then the Hyacinth, and finally the Roses. The main flowers should have a triangular relationship, with varying heights.

2. Add the secondary flowers, maintaining the balance of color and the shape of the bouquet. Add foliage and filler flowers to make the bouquet fuller (A).

3. Bend the flower stems (B) and secure the bouquet together with tape as shown (C).

4. Wrap the ribbon evenly around the flower stems from bottom to top (D, E). Tie it securely and make a bow (F). Trim off any excess ends. The bouquet can be easily inserted into a vase if desired.

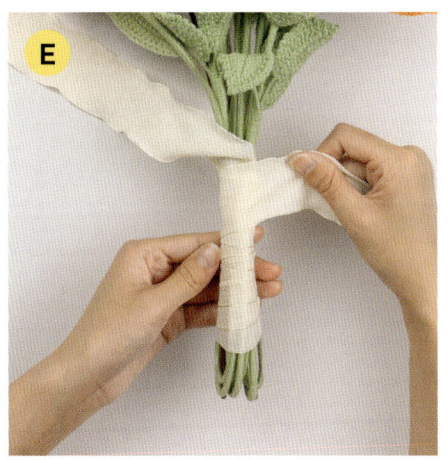

Tip

While you can use colors that complement the bridesmaids' dresses and venue decor, it's important to pick flowers that have meaning for the bride.

CLASSIC ROSES
Bouquet

Roses are a classic choice for bouquets, with red roses in particular symbolizing love, passion, and romance. This is why they are commonly given on anniversaries, Valentine's Day, and any other occasion when you want to say 'I love you'.

FLOWERS USED IN THIS ARRANGEMENT:

Classic Rose

FLOWERS

Classic Rose: 11 stems, dark red

MATERIALS

Adhesive tape

Khaki Korean-style cotton flower-wrapping paper: 3 pieces, 29cm x 29cm (11½in x 11½in)

Black waterproof floral bouquet wrapping paper: 4 pieces, 58cm x 58cm (23in x 23in)

Red ruffle ribbon: 1 x 40cm (16in) length

ASSEMBLY

1. Begin by holding a rose between your thumb and index finger. This will be the center of your bouquet. Then add other roses one by one around the focal flower. Each new rose should be placed at an angle, crossing the stems of the previous flowers in a spiral pattern. Rotate the bouquet slightly after each rose is added, keeping the stems angled consistently.

2. Once all the roses are in place, adjust them to ensure a balanced and full look. The stems should all fan out at the bottom. While holding the bouquet tightly, use adhesive tape or yarn to secure the stems where they cross at the spiral point (A). Wrap around the stems several times, making sure they're tight and secure. After tying, bend the stems evenly at the bottom to your desired length, making sure they can stand on their own if needed.

3. Fold one piece of Korean cotton flower-wrapping paper as shown (B). Place it behind the bouquet, slightly higher than the tops of the flowers, and secure it with tape (C).

4. Fold both of the remaining pieces of cotton wrapping paper in half. Pinch each center with your hand and push it up to create pleats (D). Use tape to secure a piece on each side, in front of the bouquet, at a height lower than the flower tops (E).

5. Cut one piece of waterproof floral bouquet wrapping paper in half. Take one of the pieces, fold it as shown (F) and secure it with tape on the rear side of the bouquet, higher than the inner wrapping paper. Repeat the same process on the other side, ensuring it is symmetrical (G).

6. Using the same method, continue wrapping a third layer, with the height slightly lower than the previous layer (H, I).

7. Take another piece of black wrapping paper and cut it in half. Fold it as shown (J), front and back, and secure it with tape to one side of the bouquet, positioning it below the third layer of wrapping paper. Repeat the same process on the other side – this is the fourth layer of wrapping. Using the same method, complete a fifth layer (K).

8. Tie a ribbon at the spiral point and make a bow (L). Trim any excess paper from the bottom, then tidy up the wrapping.

CONGRATULATIONS
Bouquet

Life is full of momentous occasions that reflect hard work, dedication, and perseverance. These milestones — from graduations and new homes to promotions — celebrate personal achievements and the exciting journey ahead. Flowers are cherished gifts to mark such moments and honor the recipient's efforts.

FLOWERS AND FOLIAGE USED IN THIS ARRANGEMENT:

FLOWERS

FOCAL FLOWERS

Sunflowers: 2 stems

Hyacinth: 1 stem, pink and white

Classic Rose: 1 stem, gradient pink

SECONDARY FLOWERS

Tulip: 1 stem, green yellow

Bell Flower: 1 stem, green and yellow

FILLER FLOWERS

Spray Rose: 1 stem, pink

FOLIAGE

Fern Leaf: 1 stem, green

MATERIALS

Adhesive tape

White pearl pear paper: 1 piece, 50cm x 70cm (19¾in x 27½in)

Brown Korean-style linen flower-wrapping paper: 1 piece, 50cm x 30cm (19¾in x 12in)

White water rock paper: 1 piece, 50cm x 20cm (19¾in x 8in)

Khaki honeycomb paper: 2 pieces, 50cm x 30cm (19¾in x 12in)

Pink ribbon: 1 x 30cm (12in) length

ASSEMBLY

1. Arrange the flowers and foliage, securing them together with tape. Bend and fix the flower stems in place (A).

2. Fold the pearl pear paper in half, pinch the center with your hand, and push it up to create pleats (B). Place it behind the bouquet, lower than the tops of the flowers, then secure it with tape (C).

3. Fold the linen flower-wrapping paper as shown (D) and secure it with tape on the right back side of the bouquet, higher than the inner wrapping paper (E).

4. Fold the water rock wrapping paper as shown (F) and secure it with tape on the left back side of the bouquet, higher than the linen wrapping paper (G).

5. Fold the honeycomb paper as shown (H). Secure it with tape in front of the bouquet, one on each side (I).

6. Tie a ribbon around the stems and make a bow (J). Trim any excess paper from the bottom and tidy up the wrapping. You can add your favorite stickers or cards on the wrap.

A

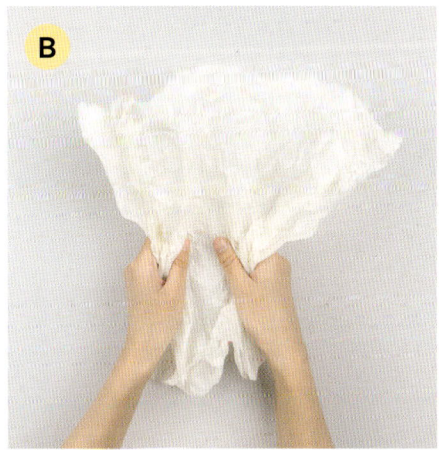
B

C

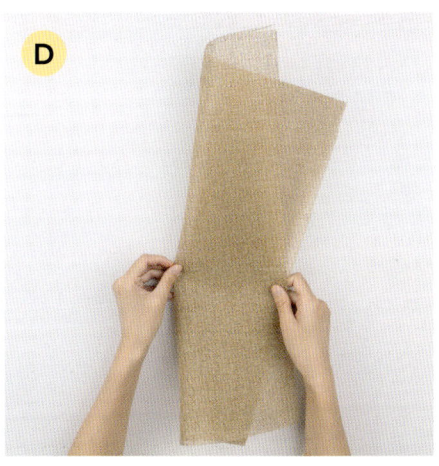
D

E

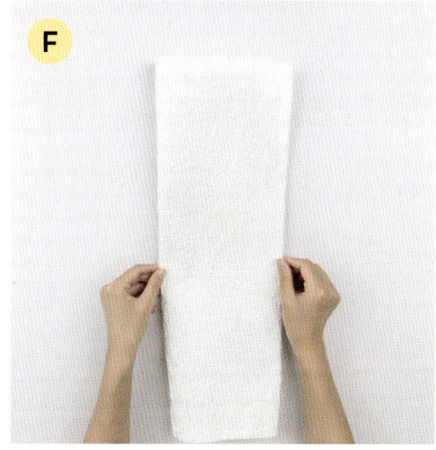
F

G

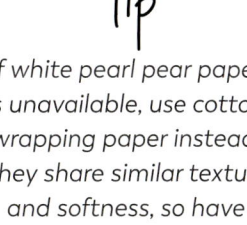

Tip

If white pearl pear paper is unavailable, use cotton wrapping paper instead. They share similar texture and softness, so have comparable visual appeal.

J

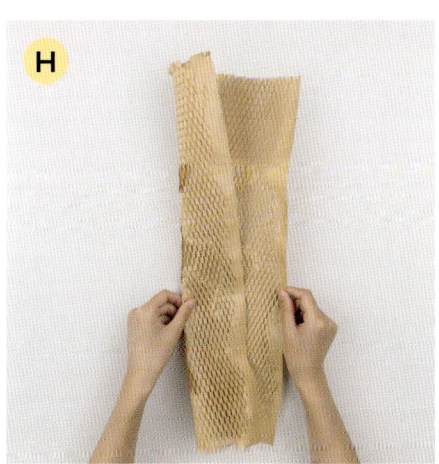
H

I

HAPPY HOME
Display

Crochet flowers, like fresh blooms, make eye-catching decorations that effortlessly brighten anywhere from the living room and bedroom to your dining table or office. As well as being permanent and maintenance-free, they have unique charm and bring lasting beauty to your space.

FLOWERS AND FOLIAGE USED IN THIS ARRANGEMENT:

White Bell Flower, Common Rose, Baby's Breath, Pink Bell Flower, Blue Bell Flower, Daisy, Northern Sea Oats

FLOWERS

FOCAL FLOWERS
Common Rose: 3 stems, pink

STRUCTURAL FLOWERS
Bell Flower: 3 stems, white; 3 stems, pink; 5 stems, blue

FILLER FLOWERS
Baby's Breath: 3 stems, white

Daisy: 1 stem, light pink

FOLIAGE
Northern Sea Oats: 2 stems, green

MATERIALS
Vase: 20cm (8in) tall, 11.5cm (4½in) upper diameter, 10cm (4in) lower diameter

ASSEMBLY

1. Begin by building the arrangement from the outside in. Define the shape and final size by placing the structural flowers (Bell Flowers), around the perimeter of the vase. Arrange the flowers to form three points of an uneven triangle (A, B, C).

2. Add the focal flowers, staggering them to create a layered effect. The big, pillowy blooms of the Common Roses add an additional layer of complexity (D).

3. Tuck in the filler flowers and foliage, using varying lengths to create movement and variety. In this step, Baby's Breath, Daisy, and Northern Sea Oats are used (E).

4. Make final adjustments to the bouquet by adding Bell Flowers to enhance its overall shape and visual appeal (F).

Tip

You can simply bend and fold the flower stems to secure them inside the vase. The staggered arrangement of the stems will provide stability. However, if you're working with flower stems that can't be bent easily, you can use chicken wire to secure the flowers in the vase.

CASCADE
Bouquet

An exquisitely crafted cascading bouquet of crocheted flowers can be customized to match the theme of any celebration. Long after the event, the delicate beauty of these handcrafted blooms will live on as a permanent keepsake, made with love.

FLOWERS AND FOLIAGE USED IN THIS ARRANGEMENT:

FLOWERS

FOCAL FLOWERS

Classic rose: 3 stems, pink

Common Rose: 3 stems, yellow

SECONDARY FLOWERS

Chinese Lantern Lily: 1 stem, orange

Cosmos: 1 stem, pink

Moth Orchid: 2 stems, white

FILLER FLOWERS

Baby's Breath: 2 stems, pink; 1 stem, white; 1 stem, orange

Bell Flower: 1 stem, white

Calla Lily: 1 stem, white

FOLIAGE

Northern sea oats: 1 stem, green

MATERIALS

Nylon zip tie (15cm / 6in)

White ribbon: 1 x 30cm (12in) length

Adhesive

ASSEMBLY

1. Start by arranging the focal flowers in a triangular distribution. This means positioning them so that they form the three points of a triangle.

2. Add greenery and secondary flower around the focal flowers, giving the bouquet a natural, elegant look.

3. Begin to form the cascading shape by positioning the Moth Orchids and Calla Lily at varying heights. Ensure that the flowers and foliage flow downward naturally (A).

4. When you're satisfied with the arrangement, bend the stems (B) and secure them with a nylon zip tie to ensure they stay firmly in place (C). Trim the tail of the zip tie and wrap tape around the bent stems, making the whole structure neat and compact.

5. Wrap the stems with white ribbon, making sure it is tight and even. Then glue it in place (D, E).

6. Make final adjustments to confirm that the cascade flows naturally and evenly. Ensure the cascade effect is visually appealing and the bouquet is secure and comfortable to hold.

A

B

C

D

E

Tip

In addition to Orchids, you can use blooms like Bell Flowers and Lily of the Valley along with slender leaves to create a cascading effect.

STITCHES & TECHNIQUES

There are several essential stitches and techniques that form the basis of most crochet projects, including those in this book. If you practice and perfect them, you will find it simple to follow the patterns and create your crocheted floral bouquet.

CHAIN (CH)

Begin with a slip knot on your hook. Hold the hook in your dominant hand and the base of the slip knot with the left thumb and forefinger of the other hand. Take the working yarn over the hook – abbreviated as yo – twist the hook counterclockwise to catch the yarn (A) and pull it through the slip knot to create a new chain stitch. Continue until you have the required number of chain stitches, gently pulling down on the chain as you go, without making it too tight.

MAGIC RING

Make a loop near the end of the yarn and hold it securely between two fingers (B). Insert the hook in the loop, yarn over, and pull the yarn through (C). Make a chain stitch to secure, then make the first round of stitches into the loop (D). Pull the yarn tail to tighten the loop (E). Slip stitch in the first stitch to join.

SLIP STITCH (SLST)

Insert the hook into the stitch from front to back, yarn over (F). Pull the yarn through the stitch and through the loop on the hook.

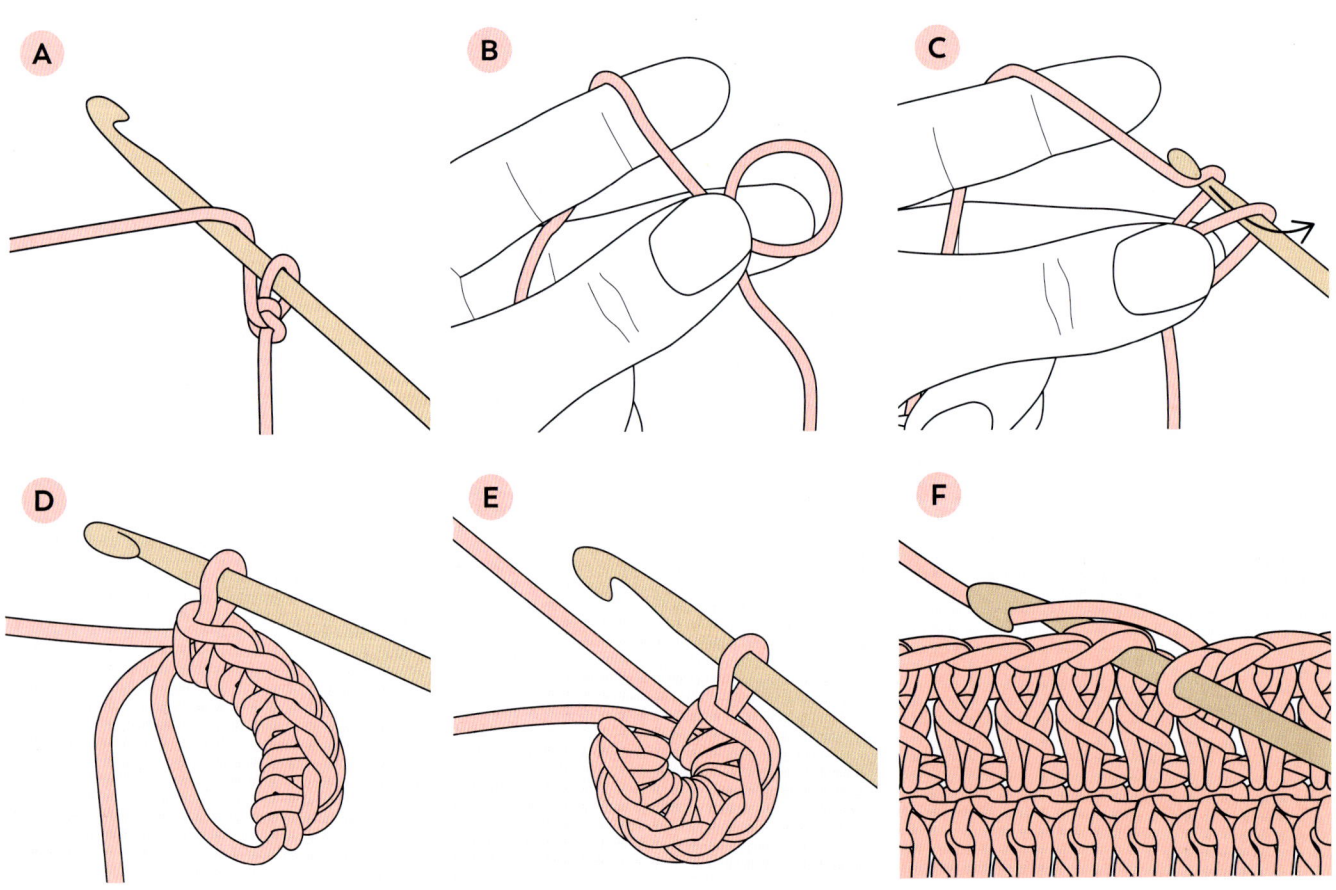

SINGLE CROCHET (SC)

Insert the hook into the second chain from the hook, yarn over and pull through the chain (G) (two loops on the hook). Yarn over again and pull through both loops on the hook (H) to complete the stitch.

HALF DOUBLE CROCHET (HDC)

Yarn over and insert the hook into the third chain from the hook (I), yarn over again, and pull through the three loops on the hook (J) to complete the stitch.

DOUBLE CROCHET (DC)

Yarn over and insert the hook into the fourth chain from the hook (K), yarn over again, and pull through (three loops on the hook) (L). Yarn over and pull through the first two loops on the hook (two loops on the hook), yarn over and pull through the remaining two loops on the hook to finish the stitch.

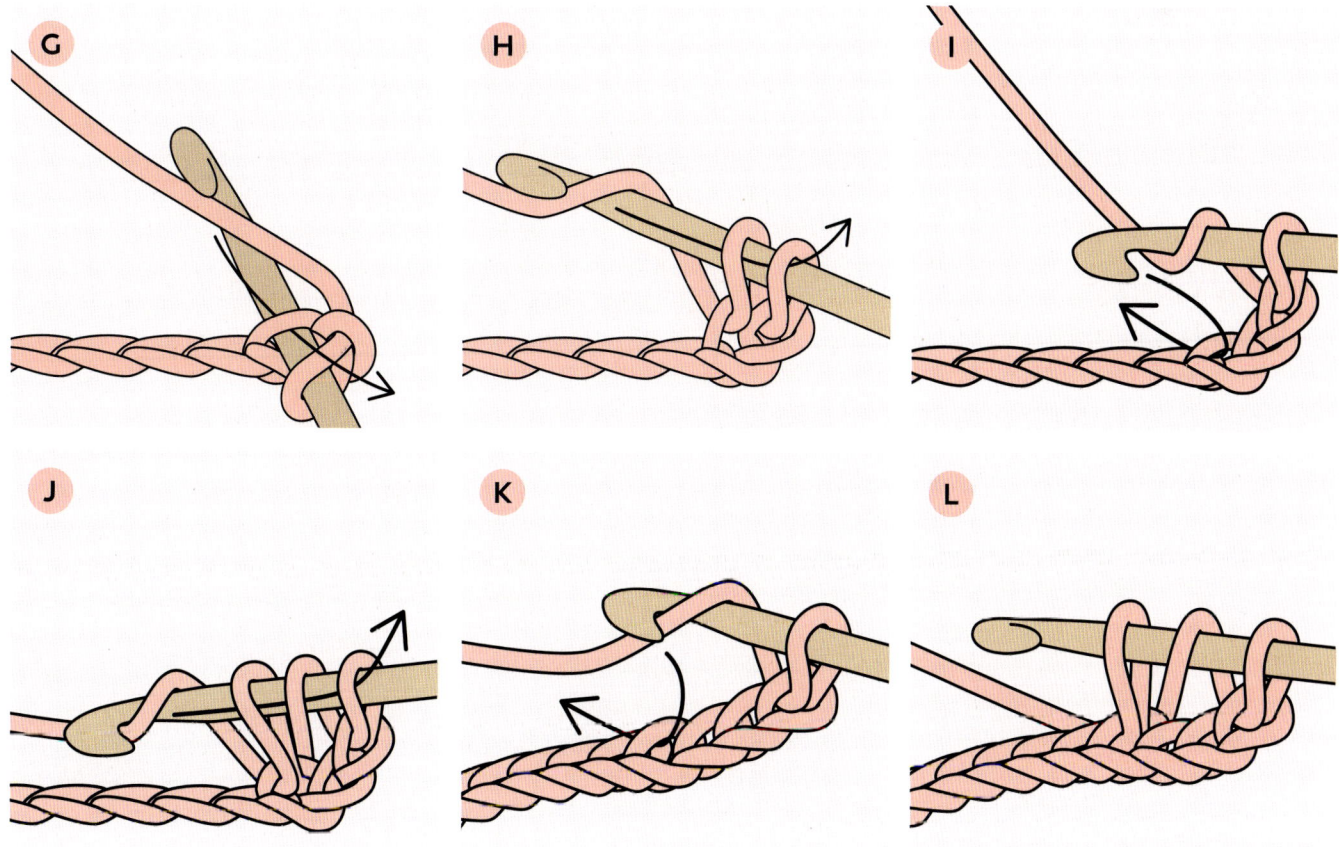

TREBLE CROCHET (TR)

Yarn over twice and insert the hook into the designated stitch (M). Yarn over and pull up a loop, now you have four loops on your hook. Yarn over and pull through the first two loops on your hook (N). Yarn over again and pull through the next two loops. Finally, yarn over once more and pull through the final two loops.

DOUBLE TREBLE CROCHET (DTR)

Wrap the yarn around your hook three times to make four loops on the hook. Insert the hook into the designated stitch (O), yarn over and pull up a loop – now you have five loops on your hook. Yarn over and pull through the first two loops on the hook, leaving four loops on the hook. Yarn over and pull through the next two loops, leaving three loops on the hook. Yarn over and pull through the next two loops, leaving two loops on the hook. Yarn over one last time and pull through the final two loops to complete the stitch.

PICOT

A picot stitch is a small decorative crochet stitch that creates a tiny loop. It is often used as an edging or to add a delicate, lacy texture to designs. Start with your base stitch and work up to the point where you want to add the picot. Make three chain stitches to create a small loop, then insert your hook into the first chain of the chain-3 (P), yarn over, and pull through both loops on your hook (Q) to complete a slip stitch. This closes the loop, forming a small bump. You can adjust the number of chains to get the different variations of the picot, for example 1ch-picot or 2ch-picot.

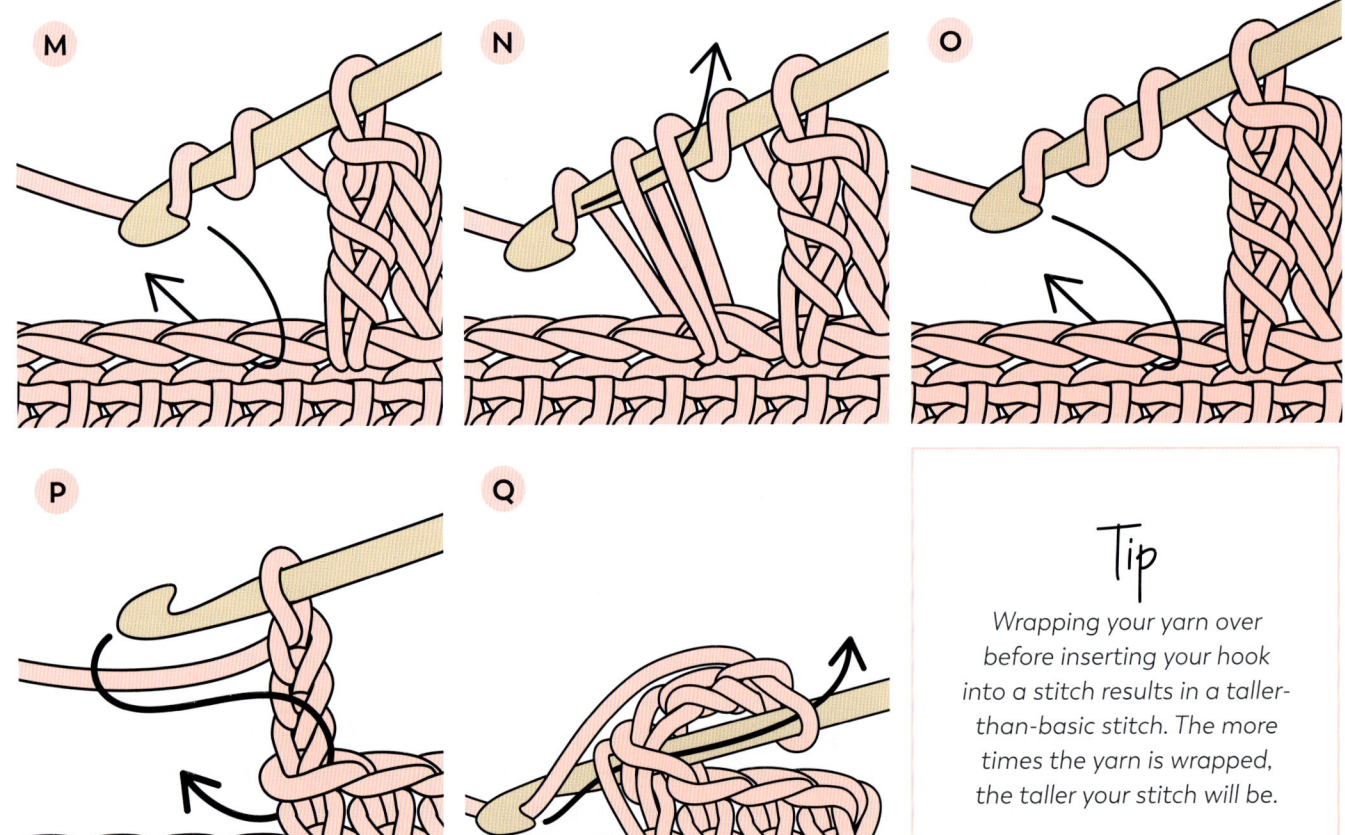

Tip

Wrapping your yarn over before inserting your hook into a stitch results in a taller-than-basic stitch. The more times the yarn is wrapped, the taller your stitch will be.

WORKING INTO THE FRONT OR BACK LOOP

These are variations of the regular single crochet where, instead of inserting the hook under both the front and back loops of the stitch, you insert it under either the front or back loop of the stitch. When looking at the top of the stitch, you'll see two horizontal loops: the front loop is closest to you (R) and the back loop is furthest from you (S).

BACK POST SINGLE CROCHET (BPSC)

This variation of the single crochet is worked around the 'post' of a stitch from the previous row. By inserting the hook from the back, you create a textured, raised effect. Look at the stitch you want to work. The 'post' is the vertical part of the stitch directly below the loops at the top. First, insert the hook around the post (T), then yarn over and pull up a loop to complete a single crochet (U).

DECREASE (SC2TOG)

This decreases by one stitch. The illustrations show single crochet two stitches together (sc2tog), but the same principle is used when decreasing using other stitches (for example, dc2tog and tr2tog).

Insert the hook in the first stitch, yarn over and pull a loop through the stitch (two loops on the hook) (V). Insert the hook in the second stitch, yarn over and pull a loop through the stitch (three loops on the hook). Yarn over and pull through all three loops on the hook (W).

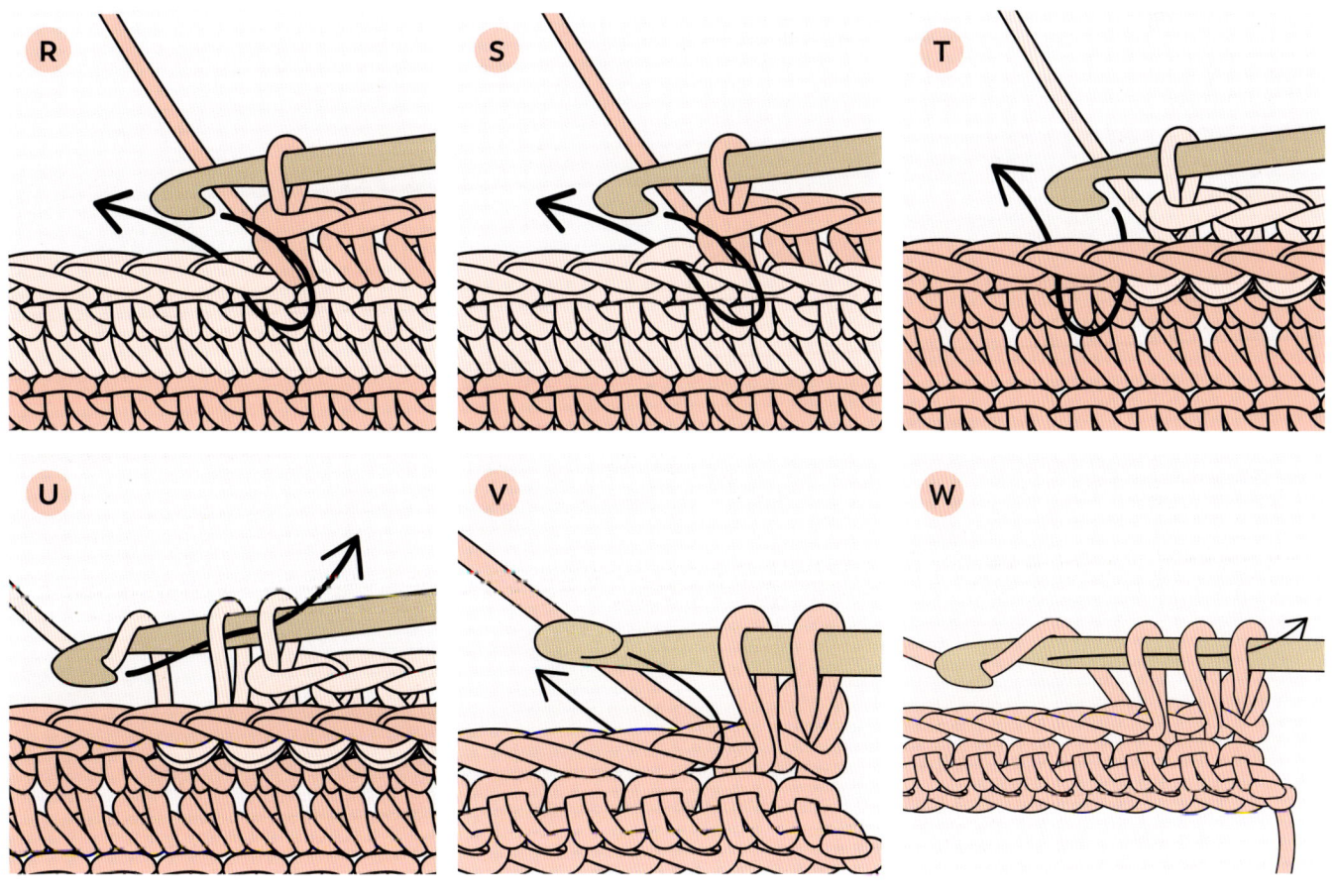

About the Author

Li Li, the founder of Lilyrosy, brings her passion for floral artistry and handcrafting together to present a unique style of environmentally-friendly crocheted floral arrangements. She's originally from China and once ran a flower shop but often felt saddened by the short-lived beauty of fresh flowers and their inevitable fading. Inspired to create a lasting alternative, she began crafting crochet flowers as sustainable gifts that retain their charm forever.

In 2022, Li Li launched Lilyrosy, a small business specializing in custom floral gifts, wedding bouquets, and decorative pieces. Her creations are thoughtfully designed to be eco-friendly, low-maintenance, and allergen-free – perfect for those who love flowers but seek a more enduring option. Through her online shop, lilyrosy.com, and her YouTube tutorials, she shares her crochet techniques, floral inspiration, and artistic journey with a growing community on social media, inspiring craft enthusiasts worldwide.

Thanks

The process of writing a book involves the support of many individuals, both directly and indirectly, and I am profoundly grateful to each of them.

I extend my heartfelt thanks to my editor, Sarah, for her exceptional insights and guidance throughout this journey. I am also grateful to Jessica and Clare for their meticulous feedback and support, which greatly enriched the content of this book.

I am deeply grateful to designers Sam and Lucy, as well as all the talented individuals involved in the editing, layout, and photography. Your collaborative efforts have made this project a smooth and enjoyable experience. I would like to recognize the crochet artists and floral enthusiasts who provided insights and shared their experiences, helping to enrich the content within these pages. Your support has been invaluable.

Additionally, I want to thank my readers for their enthusiasm and love for crocheting. Your support ignites my creativity and inspires me to continue crafting. I hope this book brings you as much joy and warmth as crocheting flowers has brought to my life.

Finally, I extend my deepest appreciation to my boyfriend and family for their unwavering support, sacrifices, and prayers throughout this journey. Without you, this book would not have been possible.

Suppliers

All materials used in this book can be found at lilyrosy.com or purchased from amazon.com.

INDEX

abbreviations 7

baby's breath 64–5, 102–5, 114–21
back post single crochet 125
bell flower 72–3, 110–21
berries, winter 60–1, 102–5
bobble stitch 51, 60
bouquet ideas 100–21
    cascade bouquet 118–21
    classic roses bouquet 106–9
    congratulations bouquet 110–13
    happy home display 114–17
    wedding bouquet 102–5
bud slices 25
buds 27–8, 37, 40–1, 43, 50–2, 54–5, 70

calla lily 74–5, 118–21
calyxes 7, 11–12, 23
    bell flower 72–3
    bud 27–8
    calla lily 75
    carnation 44–5
    freesia 37–8
    rose 11–12, 14–15, 27–8, 62–3
carnation 44–5
cascade bouquet 118–21
chain stitch 122
Chinese lantern lily 39–41, 118–21
congratulations bouquet 110–13
cordyline fruticosa 92–3
cosmos 48–9, 118–21

daisy 42–3, 114–17
decrease 125
double crochet 123
double treble crochet 124

epiphyllum 29–31, 102–5
eucalyptus
    broad 96–7
    long 94–5

fern leaf 78–80, 102–5, 110–13
filler flowers 58–75
floral stem 6
floral wire 6
focal flowers 8–31
foliage 76–99
    see also leaves
freesia 33, 36–8

ginkgo fruit 82–3
ginkgo leaf 81–3
gradient flowers 72–3

half double crochet 123
happy home display 114–17
honeycomb flower-wrapping paper 112–13
hooks 6
hot glue 6
hyacinth 16–17, 102–5, 110–13

Korean cotton flower-wrapping paper 108–9

lace 19–21
leaves
    calla lily 75
    carnation 44
    Chinese lantern lily 40–1
    common 84–5
    cosmos 48–9
    daisy 43
    epiphyllum 30–1
    freesia 37
    hyacinth 16–17
    lily 24–5
    lily of the valley 46–7
    mint 90–1
    morning glory 70–1
    peony 21
    rose 11–12, 14–15, 27–8, 62–3
    sunflower 23
    sweet pea 67–8
    tulip 35
    zephyr lily 56–7
    see also foliage
lily 24–5
lily of the valley 46–7
linen flower-wrapping paper 112–13

magic ring 122
maple leaf 98–9
materials 6–7
mint leaf 90–1
morning glory 69–71
moth orchid 53–5, 118–21

northern sea oats 88–9, 114–21

orchid 53–5, 118–21
    leaves 86–7

pearls, perforated 7, 65
peony 18–21
picot stitch 124
pistils 7, 25
plum blossom 50–2, 102–5

ribbon 104–5, 108–9, 112–13, 120–1
rose
    classic 10–12, 14, 102–5, 110–13, 118–21
    classic roses bouquet 106–9
    common 26–8, 114–21
    spray 62–3, 110–13
    Thai 13–15

secondary flowers 32–57
single crochet 123
slip stitch 122
spike stitch 92
stamen 7
    Chinese lantern lily 41
    epiphyllum 30–1
    lily 24–5
    lily of the valley 47
    morning glory 70–1
    peony 18
    plum blossom 51
    zephyr lily 57
stitch directory 122–5
stuffing 7, 45
sunflower 22–3, 110–13
sweet pea 66–7

techniques 122–5
tendrils 67, 70–1
terminology 7
tools 6–7
treble crochet 124
tulip 34–5, 102–5, 110–13
twigs 51–2, 57, 61, 66, 70

water rock flower-wrapping paper 112–13
wedding bouquet 102–5
winter berries 60–1, 102–5
working into the front/back loop 125

yarn 6

zephyr lily 56–7

A DAVID AND CHARLES BOOK
© David and Charles, Ltd 2025

David and Charles is an imprint of David and Charles, Ltd, Suite A, Tourism House, Pynes Hill, Exeter, EX2 5WS

Text and Designs © Li Li 2025
Layout and Photography © David and Charles, Ltd 2025

First published in the UK and USA in 2025

Li Li has asserted her right to be identified as author of this work in accordance with the Copyright, Designs and Patents Act, 1988.

All rights reserved. No part of this publication may be reproduced in any form or by any means, electronic or mechanical, by photocopying, recording or otherwise, without prior permission in writing from the publisher.

Readers are permitted to reproduce any of the designs in this book for their personal use and without the prior permission of the publisher. However, the designs in this book are copyright and must not be reproduced for resale.

The author and publisher have made every effort to ensure that all the instructions in the book are accurate and safe, and therefore cannot accept liability for any resulting injury, damage or loss to persons or property, however it may arise.

Names of manufacturers and product ranges are provided for the information of readers, with no intention to infringe copyright or trademarks.

A catalogue record for this book is available from the British Library.

ISBN-13: 9781446314708 paperback
ISBN-13: 9781446314722 EPUB

This book has been printed on paper from approved suppliers and made from pulp from sustainable sources.

Printed in China through Asia Pacific Offset for:
David and Charles, Ltd
Suite A, Tourism House, Pynes Hill, Exeter, EX2 5WS

10 9 8 7 6 5 4 3 2 1

Publishing Director: Ame Verso
Senior Commissioning Editor: Sarah Callard
Publishing Manager: Jeni Chown
Desk Editor: Jessica Cropper
Tech Editor: Sharon Carter
Project Editor: Clare Hunt
Lead Designer: Sam Staddon
Designer: Lucy Ridley
Pre-press Designer: Susan Reansbury
Illustrations: Kuo Kang Chen
Art Direction: Lucy Ridley and Giulia Sandri
Photography: Chen Xi, Li Rong Ha, and Jason Jenkins
Production Manager: Beverley Richardson

David and Charles publishes high-quality books on a wide range of subjects. For more information visit www.davidandcharles.com.

Share your makes with us on social media using #dandcbooks and follow us on Facebook and Instagram by searching for @dandcbooks.

Layout of the digital edition of this book may vary depending on reader hardware and display settings.